The Vital Organization

How to create a high-performing workplace

(Field Guide)

Massimiliano Ghini
Joshua Freedman

sixseconds
EMOTIONAL INTELLIGENCE PRESS

Copyright ©2015, Six Seconds
PO Box 1985
Freedom, CA 95019
Web: www.6seconds.org
Email: staff@6seconds.org
Phone: (831) 763-1800

All rights reserved. No part of this publication may be reproduced or distributed in any form or by any means, or stored in a database or retrieval system, without the prior written permission of the publisher.

Library of Congress Cataloging-in-Publication Data
Ghini, Massimiliano & Freedman, Joshua
The Vital Organization, How to create a high-performing workplace / by Massimiliano Ghini & Joshua Freedman
1. Business. 2 Leadership

ISBN: 978-1-935667-22-3

Printed and bound in the United States

Six Seconds Emotional Intelligence Press
San Francisco, California

www.6seconds.org/tools

Contents

Part I: Vitality Needed 1

In volatile markets and rapid change, what really creates organizational value? New insights from neuroscience and organizational research reveal key drivers that make the difference. These drivers define the Vital Signs model for performance.

Part II: The New Rules for Management 27

How can leaders use the new research insights to actually create organizational vitality? What are the key principles and the specific tactics that make the difference?

Part III: Case Study – Vitality in Action 69

What does it look like to put these principles into action? The Komatsu case provides a real-world example of these concepts and solutions. What are the vital lessons every leader can apply to their organization?

Notes 98

Part I

Vitality Needed

Vitality Needed :: 1

In the era of big data, does your company have a clear understanding of the factors that drive performance? Most corporate dashboards have clear metrics on cash and customers (such as sales pipelines) but a terrible deficit on the employee side. How are your people producing value? What drives them to do so, or not?

For over a decade, Gallup has tracked employee engagement[1] – commitment to put forth full energy and value. Globally, well under 1/3 of employees are engaged... and despite a decade of growing awareness, engagement levels are not increasing. In the US alone, Gallup estimates this represents wasting US$500 billion per year. Can we afford this inefficiency? Can your company reach its goals while 2/3 of the workforce is not creating real value?

Can you imagine a professional sports team where there was no clear picture of how to measure high performance? In athletics, there are detailed, specific metrics for every aspect of individual success, and professionals are selected and trained based on these parameters. Why can't this happen in business?

There are countless opinions on performance – search on Amazon.com and you'll find some 20,000 titles on this subject.[2] Yet organizational performance remains a mystery. It's time to move away from opinion and find robust data.

In 2001, Six Seconds began surveying organizations about

this topic: What drives the people-side of performance? Assessing thousands of leaders and teams in 10+ countries, we developed a database of signals of organizational performance.

What really makes the difference in uncertain times?

The US military uses the acronym VUCA to describe times like these: Volatile, Uncertain, Complex, Ambiguous.[3] In a VUCA environment, we need different strategies and tactics than in normal times (whatever those are). If we're facing new business pressures, we can't use the management approaches of the 1950s or 1980s and expect them to work today. We need an approach to management suited to today's business context.

In 2013 we launched a global research project involving more than 100 organizations and 10,000 people from different nationalities, business sectors and company sizes to understand the factors driving organizational performance today.

The good news is that we found what we were looking for! The data showed five factors, we call them the **Vital Signs**, that explain 60% of the variation in performance independent of company size, geographic location or business sector. In other words, it seems these essential factors are a common denominator for measuring performance. This relationship can be seen visually in this scatter graph:

Drivers versus Outcomes

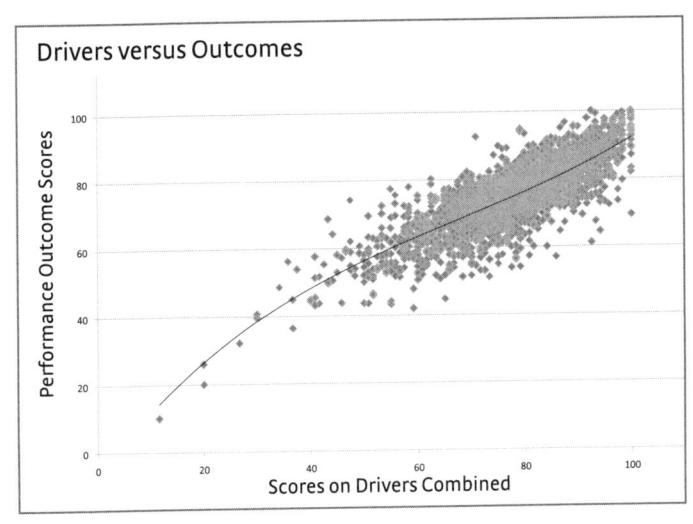

The horizontal axis is a combination of the five drivers (Motivation, Teamwork, Execution, Change and Trust). The vertical access is a combination of four key performance outcomes (productivity, retention, future success, and customer focus).

A multiple regression analysis was used to test the relationship between drivers and performance. Collectively, 60% of the variation in performance outcomes is predicted by the Vital Signs (R^2=.599).[4] That means improving the drivers is an effective approach if you want better results on these performance indicators.

A Framework for Performance

What does it mean to have high performance? What do we want in a team or organization? These questions help organize the five Vital Signs. Using the concept of a balanced scorecard, we can consider a high performing leader, team, or organization to succeed on two axes:

1. **People - Organization** (ie, individual needs vs group needs)

2. **Strategy - Operations** (ie, (long term direction vs short term action)

These can be depicted to form a simple a matrix:

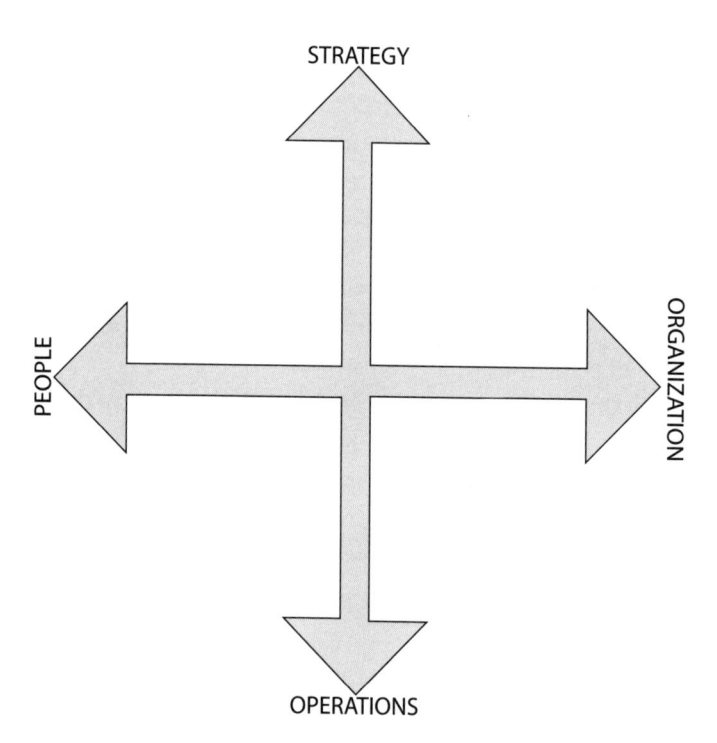

```
              STRATEGY
                 ↑
                 |
    PEOPLE ←─────┼─────→ ORGANIZATION
                 |
                 ↓
             OPERATIONS
```

We know where we're going: **Strategy**

We have systems to get there: **Organization**

We're doing the work to move forward: **Operations**

Employees are making it happen: **People**

We present these parameters on an axis because success requires the right balance – depending on the needs of the situation. Sometimes leaders, teams, or organizations need to lean more in a particular direction. For example, during an intense product launch, the focus might be more on operations. However, if you're too operationally focused for too long, you lose sight of direction. Likewise, during a reorganization, it's critical to focus on the strategy (how you will get to where you're going) and at the same time you need to maintain your customer focus (organization) – but you can't forget to communicate and engage the staff (people) or the change will fail.

For sustainable effectiveness, organizations need to balance these dimensions.

Strategy: Creating a vision of change and enrolling people in that direction.	**Operations**: Focusing the team to execute effectively.
People: Building a motivated team and enabling them to excel.	**Organization**: Maintaining focus and adaptability to pursue customers needs.

What's The Weather Like?

What kind of workplace environment will allow people to achieve these results — to perform optimally? Do you want to come work in a place that feels toxic? Or are you more likely to invest yourself in a place where you look forward to working each day?

High performing teams and workplaces share key hallmarks:

1. People have a sense of safety and assurance so they'll take risks, share, innovate, and go beyond their own comfort zones: **Trust**.

2. People need to feel energized and committed to doing more than the minimum requirement: **Motivation**.

3. They need to be adaptable and innovative: **Change**.

4. They need to feel collaboration and communicate to take on the challenges: **Teamwork**.

5. They need to be focused and accountable: **Execution**.

We can organize these Vital Signs around the performance matrix as follows:

Vitality Needed

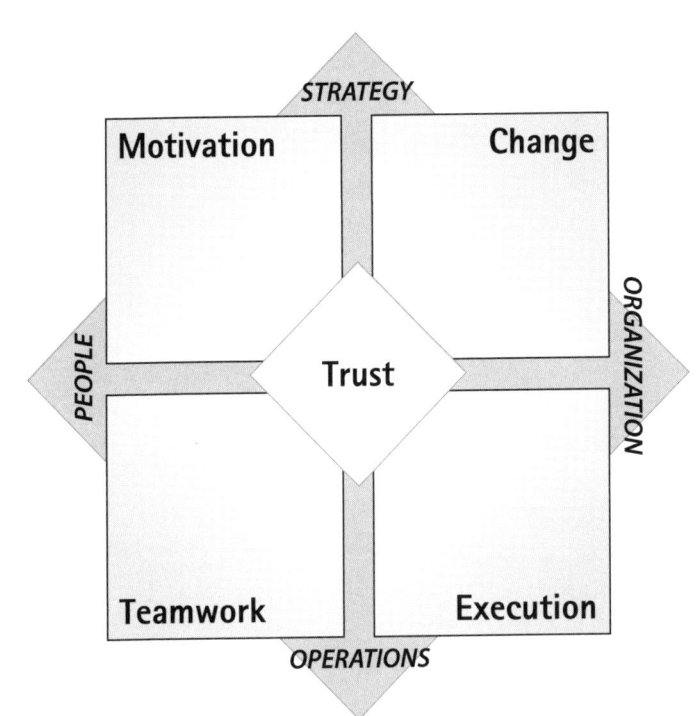

```
            STRATEGY
    Motivation  │  Change
                │
    ────────────┼────────────
    PEOPLE    Trust   ORGANIZATION
    ────────────┼────────────
                │
    Teamwork   │  Execution
           OPERATIONS
```

Motivation	Motivation is the source of energy to overcome challenges, pursue a goal, or maintain commitment.
Change	Change is the readiness to innovate and adapt to succeed in a continuously evolving situation.
Teamwork	Teamwork is collaborating to pursue a goal; it requires a sense of shared purpose and belonging.
Execution	Execution is the ability to achieve strategic results by implementing effective tactics.
Trust	Trust is a feeling of confidence, faith, and surety that engenders a willingness to risk and facilitates success in the other drivers.

Trust-Based Leadership

We conceptualize these five drivers with Trust as the fulcrum, the center. Motivation and Teamwork are on the people side; Change and Execution are on the organization side. Motivation and Change drive strategic direction. Teamwork and Execution drive operations.

Trust is the central axis of the model. Both from an empirical and a statistical point of view, we know that trust impacts on the efficacy of all the organizational (and personal) dynamics.

In this framework, we can say leadership is the ability to build a context of trust where people are highly motivated, adaptable to change, working as a team, and executing (achieving useful results).

An effective team has a foundation of trust with people who are highly motivated, open to change, working collaboratively, and getting important work accomplished.

A high-performing organization likewise has a context of trust where most staff are energized to put in discretionary effort, people are adaptable, they work together beyond their silos, and they are getting results.

It's possible to measure these drivers to get an accurate picture of what's driving and blocking performance.

From Awareness to Action

The typical response when an organization sees these results is a collective sigh – partly in relief, partly in recognition of challenge. It's validating to see the reality of the situation, even if it's not ideal. When there's a graph in the front of the room, the nebulous cloud of emotion becomes a clear picture: We know what we're dealing with.

The next question is: Can we change this situation?

The answer is YES. In Part II, we'll share the "new rules of management" that show you how. Then in Part III we'll provide a real-world case as a template for applying this insight.

Before we go to the How To, it will be valuable to lay out some key principles from recent research that offer clues to how people work. In recent years, neuroscience has revealed important insights about how the brain works. To create Vital organizations, we can tap this science to optimize people-performance.

How People Work

For years, economic theory considered the human being as "homo economicus", a rational individual who operates in markets with perfect information with respect to marginal utility. The reality that we see every day, however, is substantially different. Who has not witnessed, for example, what happens in shopping outlets with compulsive buying, "I have to have these things!" Or what about to investment decisions? The Nobel economics prize was awarded to Daniel Kahneman in 2002, a psychologist, "for having integrated insights from psychological research into economic science, especially concerning human judgment and decision-making under uncertainty."[5]

In the studies that led to the Nobel, Kahneman explored decisions to buy and sell on the equity markets. He found that when stock prices are rising, people are less inclined to assess the risk and focus on performance. When the stock prices fall, however, people are far more likely to give priority to the safety of their investments. The result is not rational: People buy when stock prices are high, run away when stock prices fall (losing money) and then take refuge in bonds (perceived to be safe but with very low interest rates). So even in a "hyper rational" situation with extensive data for decision making, the result is… Not optimal… and clearly not entirely rational.[6]

Another example happens around us every day at the office. In all the manuals of management you find rational organization of activities; managers are supposed to plan, define goals, control: all activities based on intensive analytics. Think instead of what happens in reality: how much time is really devoted to this type of rational process, and how much is used managing misunderstandings, trying to calm people, covering risk, or struggling to maintain power within the company?[7]

All this is to say, for years we've described "the world as we would have liked," while ignoring reality.[8] It might be easier if people were purely rational at work, but it's totally irrational to pretend that's the case. Confront reality: People have a rational side **and** an emotional side. If we do not put these two sides together, we will not be able to understand the actions and reactions of people.

If we try to understand people by analyzing their behavior only using rational intelligence, in many cases we are forced to say, "some people are just weird." We become convinced that it is really difficult to understand and grasp the meaning of certain behaviors. In reality, to understand people we have to add also the emotional to the rational analysis. In fact, our behaviors are influenced by what we think, but also by what we feel on an emotional level. Seeing how our brain actually works will allow us to better understand people and how to best use the potential of each.

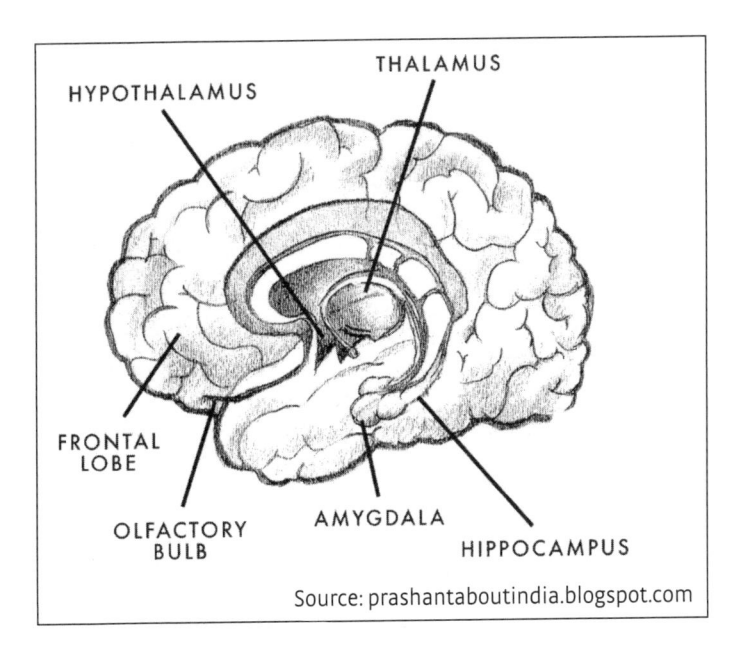

![Brain diagram showing HYPOTHALAMUS, THALAMUS, FRONTAL LOBE, OLFACTORY BULB, AMYGDALA, and HIPPOCAMPUS]

Source: prashantaboutindia.blogspot.com

Let us first define the players in the game:

> The **thalamus** could be called the "Market Research Department." It is monitoring the traffic in the brain, and constantly scanning for potential hazards.

When a the thalamus perceives a risk, it alerts the **amygdala.** This "Legal Department" is in charge of protecting us from danger pushing us to fight, flee, or freeze. It is responsible for our instinctive and primordial reactions to stay alive.

The **cortex** is responsible for rational analysis. This "Accounting Department" is assessing and evaluating the data using symbolic logic (like language and math).[9]

Let's look more closely how to better interact with these different parts of the brain.[10]

Imagine you're in a meeting, presenting an idea to the CEO. You glance over to see a colleagues' reaction. This visual data passes to the thalamus which checks: is it dangerous? If the answer is "no," the signal is then routed to the cortex for further analysis; a moment later, the signal continues to the emotional brain and amygdala to add emotional meaning to the story.

If that colleague had an expression of fear (maybe you just said something that's going to derail your project), the thalamus perceives a threat. Pay attention here: "perceives" – it doesn't mean "there is a threat," the brain's reaction is all about perception. The Market Research Team (thalamus) reacts to the danger and sends an urgent signal to Legal (amygdala), and immediately the threat response is activated. Later, the signal will continue to the cortex for the accountants to sort out the details, but once your brain perceives threat, survival becomes the driving need.

Among other things, once it comes into play, the amygdala begins to change your physiology (including increased heart rate, increased blood pressure and a mix of chemicals that will give the body energy to react). These chemicals go into the bloodstream and affect every living cell.[11]

In this moment, reality is irrelevant: whether there is <u>real</u> danger or not, your brain and whole body is preparing for battle… or to hide… or to run. When it comes to emotions, perception is more real than reality.

In addition, as you become more stressed, this whole reaction system becomes more sensitive. Stress tells that Market Research team: "Watch out, there's even more likelihood of danger now!" It's a cycle: As we increase stress, we become more sensitive to perceived threats, so we react more and pump out more of those reaction chemicals. This, in turn, makes us more vigilant for threats… and the cycle continues.

Head + Heart

What's important here is that if you want to become a leader who is truly effective in developing the Vital Signs drivers, you need a lot of insight into people and how they work. Emotional intelligence[12] is the science that provides that insight.

Emotional intelligence means being smarter with feelings.[13] It's a simple idea: Emotions are part of every person, they affect all our decisions and action. Rather than pretending we can be rational by ignoring this basic part of our neuroscience, let's actually be rational by accepting a key fact: humans are not only rational!

A popular saying the US Army leadership training center, "Leadership is a lifelong journey of just 18 inches – from head to heart."[14] It's not about giving up the rational and business intelligence that makes you successful – it's about adding emotional intelligence to the mix.

Why does emotional intelligence matter in business today?

Increasing complexity demands increased capability. If we want leaders who can navigate through today's challenges, foster innovation, and build organizations where people thrive — we need to equip them with the skills of emotional intelligence. Research shows these learnable, measurable skills improve leadership effectiveness, retention, organizational vitality, and the bottom line.

Emotional intelligence is real, it's powerful, and it differentiates top leaders from everyone else. The question is: How to use it?

Let's start with six basic principles:

1. Emotions are data

Behind every emotion we feel, there is a message.[15] If we ask ourselves "what information is this particular emotion sending me?" we improve awareness. For example, if you feel uncomfortable with a person, try to ask you what your emotions are communicating to you. Think of emotions like a car's dashboard: when your emotional "check engine light" comes on, you are receiving a signal. We have to learn to perceive our emotional dashboard lights!

For insight on the basic meanings of feelings, see www.6seconds.org/feel

2. We can try to ignore emotions, but it doesn't work!

Emotions are a psycho-physical event, they work automatically and affect our body and our mind.[16] Emotions are chemicals that exist even if we pretend they're not there. Emotions signal the body to prepare for opportunity and threat, regulating such basic functions as heart rate, blood flow, digestion, immunity, muscle response, and even body temperature. We can pretend emotions are not present, but the risk is to feel uncomfortable for long periods of time and, eventually, unfortunate effects on your health. Moreover, emotions drive our attention: They tell us what is important, they cause us to focus on certain datum. Ignoring emotions is like lying on your own eye exam: you end up with distorted vision.

3. Emotions are actually logical

While it's tempting to dismiss emotion as "random," every emotion has specific meaning.[17] It's not fantasy but neuroscience. So when we see an emotional reaction in someone, don't say "people are strange." Instead, consider that they are behaving in a way that makes sense given the emotions they're experiencing. They perceived something that made them react. Sometimes it can be difficult to see what set them off, but there is a trigger. This means we need to change our paradigm: we don't have to judge their reaction but try to understand what caused it. This is great training for leaders who want to improve relationships with their colleagues.

4. Emotions are contagious

An anxious boss often generates an anxious office – just as a cheerful and smiling teacher can put the class in a good mood and create positive conditions for learning. When we get home after a hard day and feel anxious, we need to know that our mood is going to affect the whole family. People often say that laughter is contagious; today it is clear that all the emotions are contagious.[18] Starting to take care of our emotional state is a good way to improve our relationships. Our emotions influence the response we get from others!

5. We can try to hide emotions, but not very well!

Few of us have the acting abilities of Al Pacino or Meryl Streep... if you do, probably best move to Hollywood! For most people, when we feel an emotion, others notice it. Our facial muscles contract in mouth, eyes and cheeks. We communicate the emotions we feel in that moment – at least in the first seconds.[19] Our voice changes and we may even blush. Yet all too often, we pretend that our emotions will be invisible, and enter a tense situation as if we're not broadcasting on an open microphone. For example, if we're in heated conflict and try to pretend calm, all we're doing is sending a message of distrust. If we can accept that people around us are aware of what we are feeling, we can start with reality and find a better strategy.

6. Decisions use emotions to be effective

To lose weight, for most people (excluding individuals with pathological problems), it is simple from a theoretical point of view: eat a little less and move more. We all know that, we don't have to spend money on specialists to get this information. But why is it so hard to lose weight? At a rational level we understand that losing 10 pounds would help us to play better at tennis but then in the evening we find ourselves on the couch eating chocolate. Many of us fight stress by eating, so a decision (eat less & move more) that seems clear from a rational point of view becomes impossible from the emotional point of view. To be sustainable, decisions need to be in alignment and utilize the rational and the emotional parts together.[20]

People often say that to make a good decision we should leave emotion out. It turns out, when people overuse rational thinking and under-use emotion, they actually make worse decisions.[21]

How Emotional Intelligence Works

To help people put emotional intelligence into action, Six Seconds developed a model, a process framework for accessing and using emotions effectively. Unlike other theoretical models, this is an actionable, practical, simple process that facilitates performance. The basic model is a cycle of three key pursuits:

18 :: The Vital Organization

(circular diagram with three segments: Know Yourself, Choose Yourself, Give Yourself)

Awareness (Know Yourself) - Tune into emotional data. What are you feeling? Emotions are information and we need to recognize them, identify them and be aware! Without this awareness we won't have solid basis to ground our decisions, choices and actions. Just like when you solve a math problem you need to know all the elements, to face an emotional problem you need to have all the information available.

Management (Choose Yourself) - Respond intentionally. What are my alternatives? Emotions can help direct us, but we don't want to "just react" without evaluation. We need to de-escalate and consider all the data, emotional+rational. Then we can make decisions that are emotionally sustainable and also effective. Identifying alternatives means evaluating the options that I have in order to choose what is best.

Direction (Give Yourself) - Lead purposefully. What is important for the long term? This area of the model helps to focus the choices, driving toward significance. What is actually important in this situation? What kind of person do I want to be? Am I making choices that are aligned to my goals?

So, being a leader with emotional intelligence means often asking yourself:

1. What am I feeling?
2. What are my alternatives?
3. What is important?

This process is powerful, but it's not easy at first. There are eight learnable, measurable skills that enable these three pursuits.[22]

Inside Change

The last theoretical part is about change. The traditional approach involves the need to rationally convince people of the benefits of change. Many times, however, understanding the rationale is not sufficient to actually begin change. It's important to know that every time we are about to change, or someone wants us to change, an emotional reaction arises that makes us to consider: what will happen? Will I be able to change? And if I cannot, how much energy will it cost me?

At a neurological level, one reason that change is difficult is that our brains love to follow the existing patterns. We follow these pre-existing neural pathways because:

> They are known (and what you know is less scary)

> They require less work (it's more comfortable and efficient to do what we've done before)

As a result, unfortunately, many people prefer to stay unhappily in the old situation rather than run the risk of change.

If you ask your brain to get out of the known, the secure, to go into the unknown, there is a normal emotional reaction – change is a risk. Taken from a biological point of view, this emotional jolt probably has the objective of safeguarding life, preventing you from doing something that could be fatal.

Many leaders, however, have a problem with this. They see your emotional reaction to change, then try to convince you by pushing even more on the rational side. There is a basic truth however: the more you push, the more people resist. When activated, the amygdala takes over and the rational part is of our brain not fully active.[23] In this state, all efforts to convince someone to change end up in a stalemate.

The other commonly used strategy to initiate change is fear; leaders read John Kotter's mandate to create "urgency,"[24] but they end up creating something else: "If we don't change, we won't make it through next quarter." The reaction is fear... which is very motivating. Fear motivates people to become self-protective, they start looking for new jobs, they stop sharing, they don't take risks.

Yet effective change requires risk-taking. It requires new learning, connecting, experimenting, adapting. We must break out of the old patterns and learn new ones. So, as a leader, we must ask ourselves: what can I do so to facilitate people to change?

If we can harness emotions such as excitement, courage and curiosity, we can foster engagement. Emotions then become a generative force. Feelings can help to turn the wheel, engaging change, gaining momentum. The wheel is self-reinforcing, when it moves, it produces more and more forward-moving emotions to gradually increase the speed of the change process.

In thinking about the emotional dynamics of change, it's useful to distinguish between "change" and "transition"; change is the shift itself, the transition is the psychological process that prepares us for the actual next step. William Bridges describes transition as the emotional process that comes before and continues after the change.[25]

To make change work, we developed the Change MAP.[26] "MAP" stands for "Management Process," and the model distills the latest neuroscience and theory of change into a practical and highly effective process. The secret of this MAP is to consider the emotions a valuable part of the process of change. The Change MAP provides a framework to drive transformation through three phases, shown in this graphic:

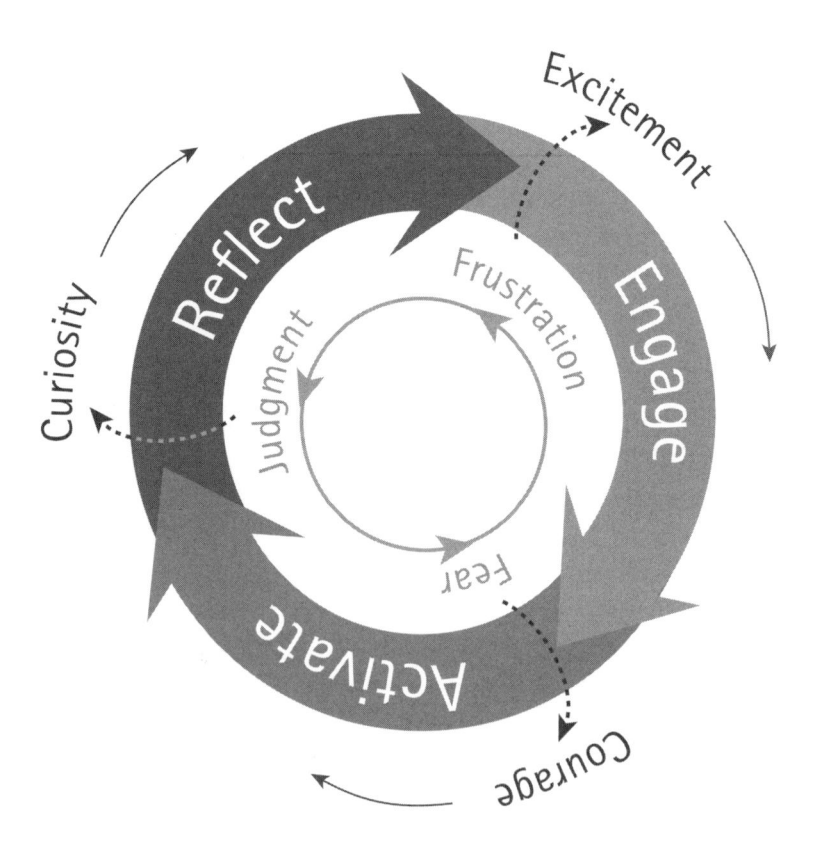

Phase 1 – Engage

In this phase, the goal is to build buy-in to a plan.

Typically this requires definition of the current status using metrics and assessments (such as "Organizational Vital Signs") to create a clear, accurate understanding of the current reality from a logical as well as emotional level. These metrics then are used to define the goals of the first iteration of the change cycle.

Since most change fails due to lack of engagement of people, this phase is all about enrollment. At a logical level, it's moving from definition to strategy. At an emotional level it's about people feeling heard, acknowledging the frustration, and building a seed of hope. People need to begin to feel that change is possible.

Phase 2 – Activate

Based on the awareness and readiness created in the Engage phase, the next step is to create new successes by generating new knowledge, attitudes, and skills. Typically, this phase requires learning — new insight to see differently, shared vocabulary to communicate about what's driving people, and new skills to build strong, healthy relationships.

In this phase, one of the key challenges is maintaining focus. A "training" is not enough to create change — it takes a process. We recommend a blended-learning approach with assessments, exceptionally powerful learning experiences, and personalized and small-group coaching to move people from awareness into action.

In this Activate phase, it's also important to build organizational capacity. While outside facilitators and coaches can be effective, to "bake in" new approaches, ultimately internal colleagues need to take up the battle cry. Using effective "train the trainer" processes and creating collaboration between outside experts and internal champions, leaders are able to develop from within the organization.

In Activate, the goal is to experience success — for people to go into action and to experience for themselves that their change is working.

Phase 3 – Reflect

The Reflect phase is about mining the previous steps. Return to the metrics collected, re-measure, identify progress. Examine the results from both logical and emotional lenses. Learn from these data; learning doesn't require success, it requires curiosity. Show ROI.

Typically, people think of change as something that is planned then executed, and that's it. In reality, we know that high performing organizations don't just make a change, they become good at change. This phase is key to that transformation because here the organization mines the successes and failures of the previous stages and then builds on those for the next round. The goal is to increase forward momentum — and accuracy.

The goal of this phase is to lock-in the wins — to be clear about the successes and failures and then to build on those to propel the change to the next level.

Recap

The data are painting a picture:

1. Performance is driven by human factors.

2. Emotions play an essential role in enabling those drivers.

3. If we are going to create change, we need to get the emotions right.

In short: Emotions drive people, people drive performance. So the leader's job is to create the emotional conditions that enable performance.

With this foundation, we can now go on to define the new rules of management, and specific tactics to put these into action.

Part II

The New Rules for Management

28 :: The Vital Organization

Given:

1. We're in times of change

2. The old rules are not producing the results we need.

3. Research shows that five Vital Signs essential drivers of performance

Then:

It's time for new managerial rules.

Since the "science of management" began to emerge in the 1950s, organizations have been structured around a command and control logic created from military tradition. The old meme was Leader as Captain of His Ship, hearkening to the days of Master and Commander on the open seas. This model was refined dramatically in the 1980s and 1990s, but the fundamental paradigm remained.

Looking at the data, and the VUCA demands we discussed in Part I, it's time to reconsider. The challenge is, almost all of us in leadership have come of age using an old model. It's familiar – so irrationally, we seek to maintain it. Instead, let's take the valuable insights and skills we've developed and put them to work in new ways:

Motivation: from extrinsic to intrinsic motivation. *Instead of carrots and sticks, managers need to understand how the brain actually works – and how people become deeply motivated.*

Teamwork: from individual to team performance. *While "stars" once created organizational value, today's business requires a dramatically different level of collaboration.*

Execution: from rigid to agile execution. *Given the rapid pace of innovation, "the perfect plan" has become a trap that actually blocks performance.*

Change: from managing to inspiring change. *Instead of a one-time change that could be somewhat controlled, now organizations need to become adaptive.*

Trust: from demanding to earning trust. *In the past, authority was respected because of position, but now leaders need to be worthy of following.*

In the rest of this section, we'll explain this pivot for the basic concepts of management, and why, given the current business reality, the rule needs to change. For each Driver, we'll provide three Pulse Points as indicators to guide this new approach,

For each Pulse Point, we'll offer three implementation examples of what it might look like in an organization.

Vital Signs Drivers and Pulse Points

You've come to the heart of this book. Below you'll find a practical guide to transforming your leadership, your team, and your organization. This isn't a recipe book, though. It's not useful to simply "follow this path," that's the old way. As you'll see below, the new rules for management require you to be authentic and adaptive. This is a tactical guide, take these methods, make them yours, and integrate them into your reality and you'll create breakthrough performance.

As explained in Part I, the drivers follow a business logic embedded in the Vital Signs Model:

```
                    STRATEGY
        Motivation          Change

PEOPLE              Trust              ORGANIZATION

        Teamwork            Execution
                   OPERATIONS
```

Below, you'll find an explanation of each driver as a "New Rule for Management," and then three "Pulse Points" as practical tactics to use to strengthen that driver. For each, we've also provides three practical examples of how organizational leaders are making each Pulse Point happen.

Motivation

From extrinsic to intrinsic motivation

The old model: people work if they receive something in return. All the theories based on motivation coming from outside (extrinsic motivation) proved themselves in a business environment focused on compliance and simplistic behavior. Pull the lever. Put the bolt in place. Do it faster.

While external motivation works for simple processes, these methods lose power when we speak about complex tasks in uncertain markets.

The new model: The VS research underlines the need for a new approach today. There are three key words linked to motivation coming from inside (intrinsic motivation). We can say M=f(VIE): Motivation is a function of: V, the value (how important it is) times I, the ability to implement (having a path forward) times E, expectation (belief in our ability to reach the goal).[27] It's not a new idea, but it's still rarely in place; Daniel Pink's recent book, DRIVE,[28] reinforces this reality.

Motivation Pulse Points

To increase motivation, develop these three key components:

1. Meaning

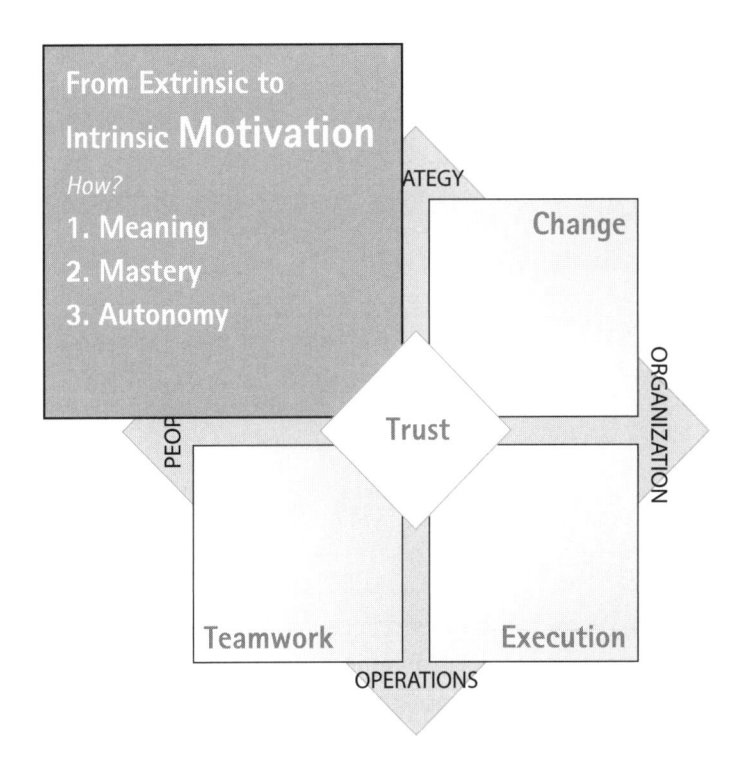

2. Mastery

3. Autonomy

From Extrinsic to Intrinsic Motivation
How?
1. Meaning
2. Mastery
3. Autonomy

STRATEGY — Change — ORGANIZATION — Execution — OPERATIONS — Teamwork — PEOPLE — Trust

Meaning [Motivation Pulse Point]

In a frenetic and fast world, people are struggling. Stress is increasing. People are losing sight of the real goal. They feel bombarded by change, especially as their companies (and bosses) keep trying new approaches.

Employees are asking...

- Why are we making this change?

- Why do we have to do what we do in a different way?

- Why do the goals keep changing all the time?

Unfortunately, all too often, the honest answer to these questions is: Senior leaders are guessing and reacting to external pressure, and people in their companies are losing sight of "the big why" – the reason we're actually here. When they disconnect from meaning, they also lose energy.

Consider this: Are you more motivated to do something:

a) important but difficult, or

b) unimportant and easy?

If we want people's energy, we need them to know, and to feel, the reason why.

So, the first responsibility of a leader is to develop a vision that people perceive as meaningful. Be careful of the word "perceived": it is not enough to write a document or make a presentation, even a brilliant one. It's not enough if it's clear to you, or to a small group. We have to give people impetus to move together in the direction that we've chosen; to do so, ensure that people understand where we want to go and why.

Take Away:

Align toward meaning; it's at the core of creating value.

Examples of Meaning in Action

1. Do employees talk about the mission & vision? Do you hear excitement in their voices, or do they mock it cynically as "corporate hype"?

2. If you ask 10 "random" people in the organization, "Why are we in business?" do you get 10 totally different answers (or, maybe worse, blank looks)? Or, do you hear a common story?

3. In a meeting to decide on a strategy or tactic, do people refer back to the mission/vision as a benchmark for the decision? (For example, "This isn't a good approach because it doesn't really align with the vision...")

Mastery [Motivation Pulse Point]

How does it feel to be inept and playing on a losing team? Do you remember in school having to play a sport in which you were terrible? How about when captains were picking teams, and you ended up chosen last? This is the opposite of motivating!

Yet in business, performance management conversations focus on "addressing weaknesses." From school, most of us learned that the way to develop is to see our faults, to see where we're failing, and fix that. All too often, a "training and development plan," or even being assigned a coach, is a message about weakness.

Working on the people's strengths is faster and more powerful. Of course we can't ignore problems; but consider a 80/20 ratio: once the person has the minimum skills required for the role, then we can focus on the strength. If someone can't add numbers in Excel, probably impossible for him to work on accounting. Once he has the basics, should we continue to focus on what he doesn't know?

Sports offers more evidence for this approach: good coaches understand their players' talents, and put them in those positions. Someone who can rocket a ball into the top-left corner of a net is wasted as a defender. It's time for leaders to do the same.

Take Away:

Identify people's strengths and play those.

Examples of Mastery in Action

1. In an annual review, how much time is spent on successes and achievements versus setbacks or failures?

2. In an employee development plan, are you trying to strengthen people talents or only to address weaknesses?

3. When forming a new team, do you identify the talents needed and look for people to match? Does anyone even know the talents of each person inside your organization?

Autonomy [Motivation Pulse Point]

How does it feel when others are controlling you and you have no choice? Today, people at work want to have a sense of empowerment and freedom to choose. On the job, we are adults, and we feel more fulfilled in work if we perceive that we are captains of our own ships. It can be frustrating, to lead a team of these captains (especially for older and more traditional managers). It's easy to think, "we're paying you, so just follow my orders!" But the most successful organizations don't want employees to just do as told, they want employees to give more; and want their full commitment.

To make this shift, we need to give people the objective and be open to multiple solutions they use to reach it. This approach means an increase in questions instead of statements. Sometimes this open approach is slower to reach a decision, but in the end, involvement creates motivation that lets people go far faster. Of course, involving people in the decision is not always possible, but every time we can, make the opportunity to raise people's intrinsic motivation.

Take Away:

Give power and space for people to make decisions and own the results.

Examples of Autonomy in Action

1. When launching a project, are participants handed a detailed action plan or, instead, is there a clear goal and space for collaborators to create their own plans?

2. Are your employees rewarded if they reach goals or if they follow the rules?

3. Are your employees free to schedule their working time? Is there space in the year for them to set their own priorities and innovate?

Teamwork

From individual to team performance

The old model: Identify star performers; promote and reward them. "How" you hit your target doesn't matter, just reach the number. Even if someone is leaving a trail of destruction behind them, if they're getting desired results, they're a star.

The new model: In a complex world, it's difficult for just one person to have a complete vision. Results in today's business don't really come from individuals, and increasingly breakthrough innovation is the responsibility of divergent teams. More and more, performance is explained by our capability to work with others to solve problems and create synergies among multiple talents.

The strength of a real team is superior than the sum of the individuals. For this reason companies have started considering that individual evaluations aren't enough anymore. If we want real collaboration, we need to change the way we support and evaluate performance so both are shared. "How" results are achieved becomes essential — individuals are responsible not just for personal objectives, but for creating the conditions where the group excels.

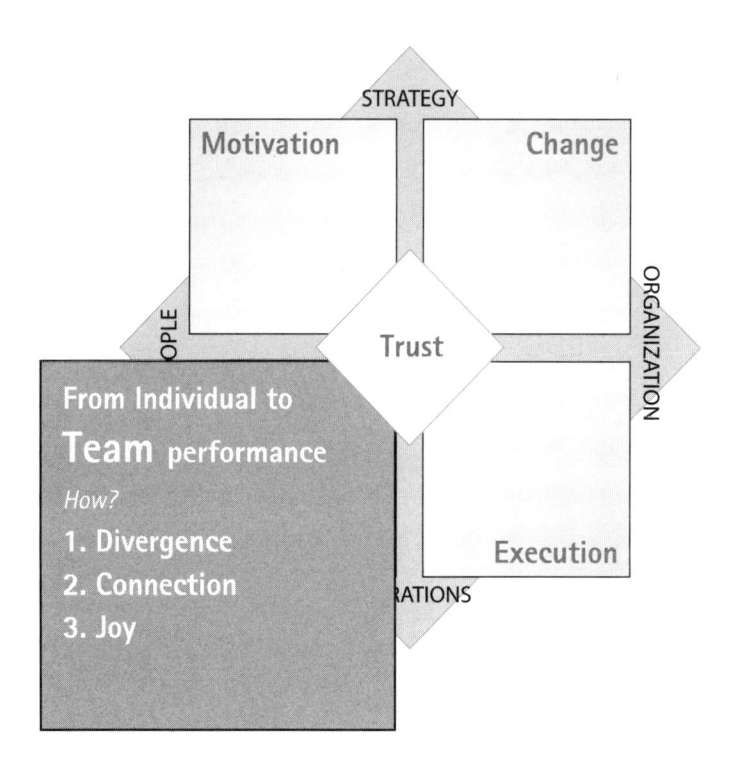

Teamwork Pulse Points

To increase teamwork, develop these three key components:

1. Divergence
2. Connection
3. Joy

From Individual to Team performance
How?
1. Divergence
2. Connection
3. Joy

Divergence [Teamwork Pulse Point]

The risk, especially for the successful people, is to remain a hostage of the past. If you always used certain methods that brought you success, your brain is tempted to propose again that winning scheme. The result: You don't innovate. If the world is unchanging, this is fine. Unfortunately, as Paul Valery said, "the future isn't what it used to be;"[29] we are in times of chaotic change!

Having "divergent" people around the table may help us to exit from known patterns. Even listening to different ideas can help the leader and group by sparking new neural synapses that can lead to different solutions. Simply sharing ideas among similar-thinking people actually reinforces bias, which is a big risk with brainstorming[30] without real divergency. The term "divergent" is beyond diverse, it's about engaging multiple perspectives and style – from age, gender, ethnicity, experience, and brain style. This range helps us to face challenges with more capability to understand the complexity of the situation and produce original or breakthrough solutions.

It's more comfortable to be with people who are "like you," who think in similar ways, who reinforce your assumptions, in fact our brains seek this confirmation. However, working with a team of people who think in different ways, who bring different experiences and perspectives, will create dissonance. That may make our brains less comfortable, but it's essential to break out of the old patterns.

Take Away:

Value, and seek out, contrasting perspectives in order to shift out of old ways of thinking.

Examples of Divergence in Action

1. In a meeting, what happens when someone expresses a dissenting view? Is it met with curiosity, or shut down?

2. Are decisions made based on what's already known, or are people seeking out multiple perspectives? (e.g., A-B testing)

3. In selection, are hiring managers actively seeking candidates who will be an "easy fit" or those who will add something new? Are your teams formed on Divergence (different talents, background, brain styles) or on expertise?

Connection [Teamwork Pulse Point]

Is every group who works together a team? What's the essential ingredient that makes the title of "team" appropriate? Prerequisite for "teamness" are a common challenge and a sense of belonging that makes the members say "Us."

When people feel connected and have that "us" identity, they are more open to share information, to collaborate, and to invest energy. There's a primal human drive to be "in" the group, this creates a bond and mutual commitment to survive and thrive.

To make "team" happen, build a culture where people share, not just at a rational level, but emotional one as well. Remember connection isn't just a question of logic. This requires increasing awareness of emotional dynamics. It's helpful to have a shared vocabulary for talking about relationships, emotions, and culture. Consider: how does it feel to be in this group? Feelings such as appreciation, acceptance, curiosity, caring, and calm will fuel connection, which will in turn fuel "teamness."

Take Away:

Feeling connected is a driver of "team" – and it's not just logical.

Examples of Connection in Action

1. Do almost all team members actually know one another, or are relationships at a surface, "professional," level only? Do team members look forward to collegial social activities or dread them? If they see one another on the street would they stop and chat, or pretend not to see one another?

2. To what degree do key influencers invite others to join (vs. maintaining separate cliques)? Are all members of the "team" invited to share perspective?

3. Are you frequently asking about and acknowledging team members' feelings? Do you measure, and work to improve, the team climate?

Joy [Teamwork Pulse Point]

The teams that obtain the best results are also those who have fun. Again, we crash against the bias that work is "serious," and therefore unpleasant. Let's not confuse "serious" with "boring."

Think about a sports team or a drama club or any other group you've loved being part of. Chances are, there was discipline in equal measure with laughter. Humans are wired to be social, and joy is a biological signal of connection and thriving. Even in the most "rational" parts of our brains, dopamine receptors provide reward circuits to reinforce actions that create joy. As neurobiologist Candice Pert discovered: We're wired to feel good.[31]

If people don't have fun doing what they do, unfortunately they will use only a part of their potential and of their brain. The newest neuroscientific research reveals that anxiety, frustration and boredom drive our brains to produce chemicals that reduce key capabilities to reflect and create meaning.[32] This reduces our thinking potential. These chemicals are signals of risk and danger, and push the human brain to short-term, protective, pattern-driven thinking, and narrow our attention to attend to problems. This is a recipe for disaster in a market driven by collaboration and innovation.

Using joy doesn't mean that you have to create a playground for your employees. In fact, real joy is not triggered by superficial inducements like the iconic Silicon Valley foosball tables or bicycles on campus.[33] Rather, the point is: focus on people's moods. Create exciting challenges for those who want to engage; make it enticing for those who want to play. When possible, ensure the team includes people who feel passionate about the work at hand, not just possess highest technical expertise. This may require re-thinking selection to move from conventional hiring for task skills, and dramatically increase a focus on process skills.

Again in sports, it's easy to see adults working hard at play. Why not try to recreate similar situations at work?

Take Away:

When people love what they're doing, they engage more deeply individually, and with one another.

Examples of Joy in Action

1. During meetings and team work sessions, do you hear jokes or pranks? Can you do serious work while maintaining a light tone? Do you see high energy and playfulness in your teams? Do your leaders have tools and practices to work on the emotional side of business?

2. In a culture of possibilities, people can try to achieve challenging goals and experiment with new ideas. New projects are assigned to people who like to innovate and have the process skills for creating a positive team.

3. Are your people chained to their desks? The brain needs physical movement to access full potential, so create a working environment where people can move and think.

Execution

From rigid to agile execution

The old model: Define a standard operating procedure, and rigorously follow it. Fine tune to eliminate waste, and repeat the same process with increasing consistency. This is the culmination of Kaizen and Six Sigma which pioneered in manufacturing, then extended to all types of business in the 1980s and 1990s.[34]

The old model is akin to planning a trip across the country by taking out books and maps, and drawing a route that will be followed without revision. Now we have GPS in our cars and phones, and we can update directions on the fly. If there's traffic, or construction, or we see an opportunity, we're free to re-route and update the path in seconds.

The new model: Set a clear strategic direction, then use a rapid-prototyping logic to iterate, improve, and adapt. The process of Agile software development is an excellent example: While holding an end goal in mind, take small, clear, effective steps with high accountability and ownership.

In most businesses, execution today is radically different from a generation ago. Once it was meaningful to commit to a five-year development cycle, now we need to adapt to a rapidly changing reality. As such, people need clear goals and real empowerment to meet those – to follow what the military calls, "Commanders Intent" when the original plan falls apart (which it always does). For example, most companies are now finding the process of yearly goals and budgets meaningless. Instead goals and plans need to be reviewed and updated on the fly.

Execution Pulse Points

To increase execution, develop these three key components:

1. Focus

2. Accountability

3. Feedback

Focus [Execution Pulse Point]

As complexity increases, the risk is increased chaos. There are more and more variables to consider. If one is attempting to track 17 objectives, at the end of the day, it's as good as having none; it's impossible to prioritize and decide where to put your resources. We suggest the "magic number" is three. There's something easy and effective about three priorities, perhaps that's why the "tricolon" is so widely used in rhetoric.[35] Each of these 3 key current goals should be broken into "chunks" and each chunk needs to be achievable within a month.

Successful leaders support their people to turn meaningful goals into concrete actions.[36] Otherwise, uncertainty

The New Rules for Management :: 47

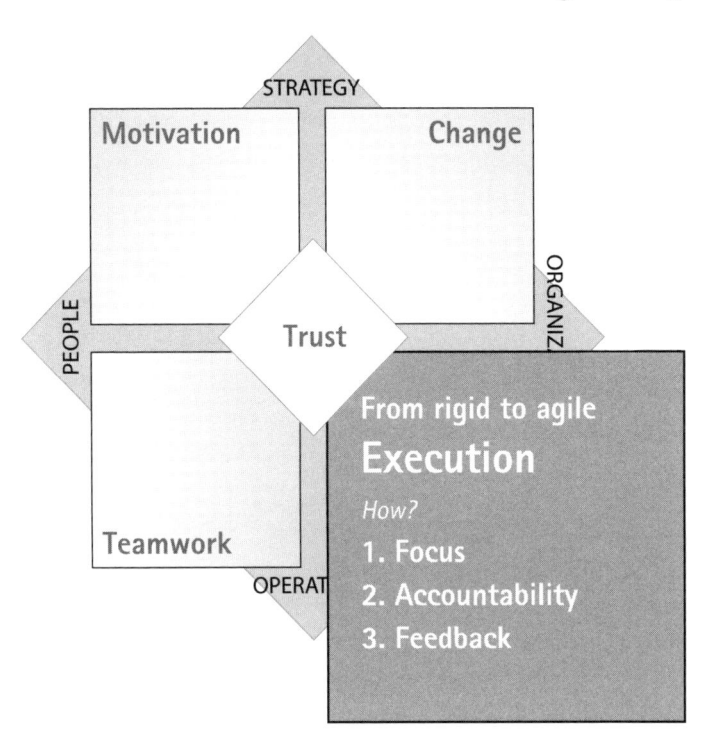

```
                    STRATEGY
         Motivation          Change


   PEOPLE              Trust           ORGANIZ

                              From rigid to agile
                              ### Execution
                              *How?*
         Teamwork             1. Focus
                    OPERAT    2. Accountability
                              3. Feedback
```

creates a lack of action, which breeds frustration and anxiety. Then we're back to the cycle of resistance, with thinking narrowing and defenses rising.

Finally, in an uncertain world, every three months we need to have to chance to review the goals and the actions to update them. This update needs to be based in reality – not trying to "look good" against a yearly target.

Take Away:

While moving toward strategic goals, define three specific, actionable priorities each month.

Examples of Focus in Action

1. Do all the people inside the company know the three main goals we are standing for? Are we all running to achieve the same objectives?

2. Are the performance goals revised frequently during the year as priorities change? In an uncertain environment you need at least a meeting per quarter to see if, due to the new business conditions we are experiencing, we need an update or a change of the goals.

3. If an emergency arises do we have systems to refocus the organization quickly? Have we considered in the organizational design how to face the ordinary and extraordinary challenges? In modern organizations, we need to work on efficacy and efficiency at the same time.

Accountability [Execution Pulse Point]

In the VUCA[37] business context, multiplied by a scarcity of truly strong talent[38], we need something different. We want speed and adaptability, and we want people to feel ownership of their work. So, let's actually give them that ownership. But with ownership of the choices comes ownership of the results.

Create a clear scope of work, define success, and delegate. Effective delegation requires specific, clear criteria on which success is measured; negotiate mutual agreement on these conditions and a realistic timeline. Then make space for people to work.

We must assess performance against the agreed upon criteria. Note that accountability does not mean "punishment." If you want to maintain innovation and energy, don't stigmatize failure: use it for learning. If the individual or team didn't reach the agreed results, mine that, understand that, work from it. While some organizations see "accountability" as, "we know who's to blame," a real culture of performance can be obtained if the focus is on improvement and excellence. That doesn't mean tolerating ongoing under-performance. It does mean setting a tone that encourages risk-taking and open, honest appraisal of success and failure.

Take Away:

Let people choose and make the results clear. Then, right or wrong, treat every choice as an opportunity for learning.

Examples of Accountability in Action

1. If a manager "does the right thing" for a customer or for ethical reasons, but it costs the company money, will he be punished or face a financial loss? In other words, is my reward system built on the assumption that we are leading in uncertain times?

2. Do we celebrate failure, or only success? If our culture is based on punishment of errors, we have a problem: the risk is that people will maintain conservative targets instead of trying to do their best

for excellent results.

3. If an employee is empowered to make a decision, is she actually free to do so? Or does she perceive that she has to check with supervisors? If she knows that she'll be blamed when a supervisor disagrees, she doesn't actually have the power, which means she isn't actually accountable.

Feedback [Execution Pulse Point]

Closely tied to accountability is the need for visibility. Ideally, in real-time, from moment to moment, all performers would be able to see their current results. Constant, clear data provides a shaping force to calibrate and refine performance.

Again, athletics offers a fitting example: if you have a game each week, at the end of the hour there's a score. It is visible to everyone, so all team members know where they stand. This creates alignment and focus on what needs to be accomplished. In managerial terms, an accurate benchmark lets us make meaningful comparisons to understand where we stand and what's needed ahead.

There's a risk here to get trapped in old patterns and just try to improve performance in an incremental way. In a chaotic market, while we're trying to eke out a 3% improvement, someone else will come along and pivot, creating a whole new approach that puts us out of the market. So, don't create data tracking and benchmark systems measuring what's easy to see. Instead, measure what is important.

We often say, "what you measure is what you get." Be sure you're measuring what matters.

Take Away:

Provide performance data that's visible, timely, and meaningful.

Examples of Feedback in Action

1. Do all your employees know the situation? Do you have an intranet or a screen where every employee can see if we are on target or not? Do you use a clear system such as a color code to make it easier to get feedback?

2. Do you measure only data that's easy to get, or what is most important? Almost all companies measure cash flow frequently; few companies are looking for meaningful people metrics with the same intensity. For example, what if your intranet included a weekly mood tracker? It's a must to understand the emotional status of people; as we know: emotions drive people and people drive performance.

3. Is feedback useful or pro-forma? In some orgs there's too little, in some there's too much, and in almost all it's 'picky' instead of meaningful. Does feedback come top-down, or also peer-to-peer and bottom-up? In a culture of healthy feedback, there is an ongoing, multi-sided dialogue about improving what's important.

Change

From managing to inspiring change

The old model: To drive organizational transformation, every few years, or even every few decades, a small team develops a complete, logical plan for the change process. Then, managers make it happen, and once done, the change is complete.

Many, if not all, organizations face a different reality today. Leaders are now asking, "What's the change of the day"? Change isn't happening every few years, it's happening continuously – and "change plan #237" is probably still underway when it's time to start working on plan #238.

The new model: Increase the capability to change by ensuring people have the skills, awareness, and attitude to make it happen. Rather than change from a plan (probably written by a consulting firm), people across the organization, horizontally and vertically, need to engage. Change makers need to win minds and hearts.

Through this lens, we see why leaders need to be coaches as well as strategists. They need to understand how people actually work – starting with the brain. Neuroscience suggests change is a process of learning new schemes; creating a new "map" to update the old one.[39] To be effective in that process, our brains need three things: repetition, curiosity and the right mix of emotions. The leader must become a full time change manager, bridging the business demands with the reality of how the human brain works best. If you see similarities with the Change MAP[40], you are right...

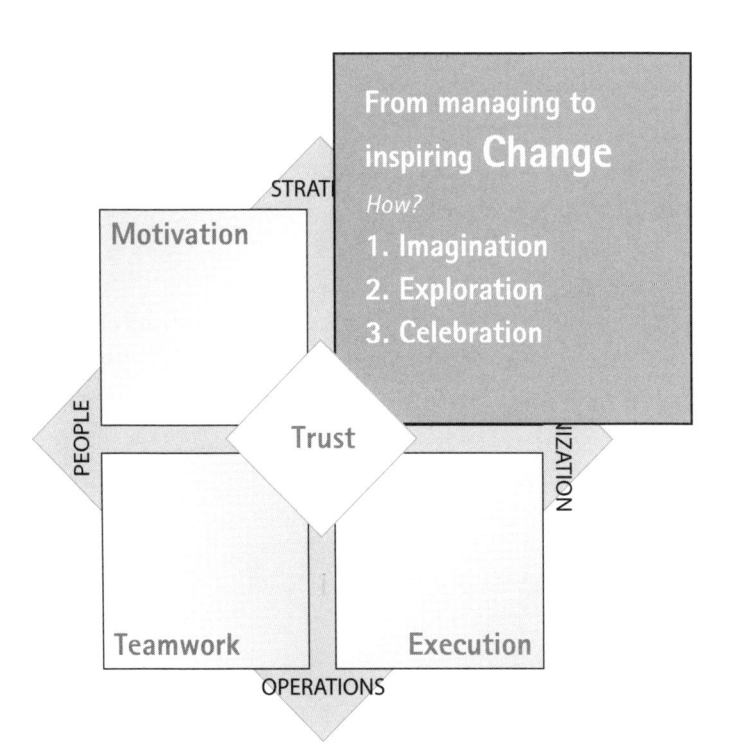

Change Pulse Points

To increase change, develop these three key components:

1. Imagination
2. Exploration
3. Celebration

From managing to inspiring Change
How?
1. Imagination
2. Exploration
3. Celebration

STRAT[
Motivation
PEOPLE
Trust
NIZATION
Teamwork
Execution
OPERATIONS

Imagination [Change Pulse Point]

Is a small incremental improvement enough? In an era where industries are revolutionized, where computer makers overturn communication giants, and startups raise millions on a Kickstarter campaign, will another 3% improvement guarantee your company's place?

If we want innovation, it starts by fostering a delight in getting out of the box. There are many reasons this is difficult. Traditional hierarchy resists innovation, especially ideas that somehow overturn embedded power.[41] In a culture where knowledge is power, and high-status people are "right" even if not insightful, it's unlikely that any truly new ideas will get a hearing. This means we need to actively seek out different, even contrary perspectives and continuously ask, "What if...?"

Even in a flat startup, our brains join that resistance. To save energy, the brain creates patterns – like a subroutine that's called quickly and easily. It becomes comfortable, it "feels right," to follow those pre-existing pathways. The risk is, patterns unconsciously hold us prisoners of our own past experiences. We don't see outside the walls of our own comfort. Worse, the more we feel stressed, the more strongly our brains will insist on the codified solutions.[42]

In order to activate a process of imagination, we need positive energy. We need to feel safe, open, curious and adventurous. It's especially challenging to get the right mood during times of economic challenge or when facing the realities of business pressures. This requires a healthy organizational (or at least team) vitality, and emotional intelligence.

Take Away:

Create a positive mood, invite and support out of the box thinking, and seek alternatives.

Examples of Imagination in Action

1. When you want to find a solution to a business problem, are you engaging teams in parallel pilots to experiment before deciding for the whole org? Ask people if they want to be part of an innovation team. Accurately gauging the mood of the people is crucial to the results. Make it an option and select only those who are willing to participate. Use Design Thinking or Agile to create rapid prototyping and experiment.

2. What happens when someone challenges a basic assumption or dares to imagine a new path? Do leaders jump on them, or do they have the skills to create the emotions to facilitate innovation?

3. Do you accept the "known answer" or are people expected to find multiple perspectives? Expose your team to business cases from different sectors or success stories from interesting people. You can stimulate associative thinking and the production of new ideas for your company, and actively look "out of the box" to increase imagination.

Exploration [Change Pulse Point]

Let's go back to an 18th Century naval frigate. They're sailing the high seas, when suddenly a pirate comes into view, and there is going to be a battle. Our sailors run out the guns and fire a blistering broadside. None of the balls hit. Problem? No. They reload, and using the experience from the first salvo, adjust, and fire again. Now a few shots hit... and with each cycle, they get better. The bad guys strike their colors, and our side wins.

Can we apply the same paradigm to modern business? Rather than seeking a "perfect" plan that paralyzes us in pursuit of that perfection, let's do a prototype and then refine. Rather than endlessly planning – creating long documents full of projections that are even more fictional than our story about the pirates – we need an adaptive process for planning. The US Navy calls it an 80% Solution. Get close, then get closer.

This "Ready-Fire-Aim" process also is also very useful for training our brains. We condition ourselves to take the risk, to jump in, try, and then adjust. That is a process we could also call, "learning."

Of course the "Aim" phase is critical – we can just keep guessing. We need a little preparation, a test, and then time to refine. This cycle produces energy, creativity, and the opportunity to explore. To test. To see what might work better.

Take Away:

Adopt an experimental approach of, "Ready, Fire, Aim," where new initiatives can quickly be put into action, tested, and refined.

Examples of Exploration in Action

1. When you want to start something new, do you create "space" for that? Or is it added to the workload of over-busy people who are immersed in their "regular work" as well? For example, create a startup team with 90 days to be 100% dedicated to launching a new prototype.

2. Do you create multiple prototypes? In an uncertain world you need multiple options. In Silicon Valley, only two out of 100 start ups will be a success. So prepare different prototypes, don't play just one game but engage more teams to have a wider pipeline of experiments. If possible, when you are 80% ready (in a world like ours you'll never be 100% ready), launch the product or service in beta version to continue to refine based on the feedback.

3. Are your meetings constantly rehashing the same issues? Can you empower different people to lead different meetings, based on their strengths and unique insight? What happens if you focus on a topic, go out in the world and see multiple ways of working on this issue, then come back and share your findings?

Celebration [Change Pulse Point]

All too often, organizations have started a new initiative before the dust has settled from the last round. The battle cry of the beleaguered planner: "We don't have time to talk about last week, we need to focus on tomorrow." Or, the perfectionist: "That was well done, but let's not take our eyes off the prize, we have to improve more this quarter..."

There are multiple reasons for this impatience. One core factor is the scarcity of time. Under intense pressure to do-more-with-less, managers are reacting rather than planning. There's also a fear of complacency, and a misassumption that celebrating success will make people stop working hard.

Perhaps the biggest obstacle is fear of conflict and controversy. "What if some team members are unhappy with the project? We'll have to deal with all that messy emotion." So, the manager jumps into the next round, hoping that people will simply leave their frustrations behind. It won't work.

If we want to be effective in change, we need to step out of the daily frenzy and review what's working, and what's not. Without judgment or blame, we can acknowledge failures and learn. Then, we can celebrate success, and even celebrate the learning from the failures.

Celebrate means investing time to acknowledge the efforts that have gone into the work thus far. Value the failures by learning, and enjoy the successes by appreciating. The celebration creates energy that then fuels the relaunch the next round of challenges and goals.

Take Away:

Find the value in what's happened recently, whether success or failure. Acknowledge, appreciate, learn, and then step into the next round.

Examples of Celebration in Action

1. Do you invest time debriefing after a project? The reality is we usually find time for the briefing but almost never for the debriefing. Start by gathering people's perceptions; don't assume that everyone on the team is feeling the same about the project.

2. One of our clients has a prominent "Failures Showcase" with key lessons-learned from those bad experiences. It's useful to underline that every failure is an opportunity to learn.

3. Have "celebrations" become obligatory and boring? Avoid an established routine; if it's formulaic, you lose spontaneity and diminish curiosity and energy. Value the principle of celebration, then ask your people to use their imagination to create something new to recognize progress, say "thanks" to people and their families. The only limit is your creativity.

Trust

From demanding to earning trust

The old model: Leadership is a process of controlling. "Do as I say." In this model, rules and policies are essential drivers. The expectation is that people are lucky to work for you, and for this privilege, they had better follow you.

From an organizational perspective, create the "spin" and

people will see the organization and its leaders in a rosy light. This makes it important to limit information and package the image. Organizations are trusted because they "look right" and it's "normal" to adjust accounting, adjust messaging, and adjust appearance to create that picture.

Either fortunately or unfortunately, today social media means everyone is a spokesperson and millions of people can see every comment. People work in open spaces, technology provides instant visibility to what's really happening, regulations demand greater transparency to the real numbers, and it's hard to hide. "Spin" still affects perception, but authenticity is more important.

At the same time, younger workers are not willing to follow arbitrary rules and hierarchy "just because." Once leaders were followed because they had the title. Now, especially with millennials, role-based power is becoming weaker.

The new model: Leadership is a process of being a role model. People are watching, and employees will do 30% of what you say, but 70% of what you do. Every day you're on the playing field, you are earning or losing trust – and trust is the currency of emotional capital. It is the lifeblood of the emotional economy, a determining factor in all the other Vital Signs. With trust, people will take the risk to change, to work together, to dig deeper, and to go further. Without it, they'll hold back.

In addition, trust is contagious: a leader that doesn't trust his coworkers will rarely gain his team's full trust. Distrust is a signal of un-safety, at a primal level our brains are on the lookout for this kind of danger: If you don't have my back, I won't take the risk to have yours. For good or ill, it's

Trust Pulse Points

To increase trust, develop these three key components:

1. Transparency
2. Coherence
3. Care

From demanding to earning Trust

How?
1. Transparency
2. Coherence
3. Care

Motivation — Change — Teamwork — Execution

STRATEGY — ORGANIZATION — OPERATIONS — PEOPLE

Transparency [Trust Pulse Point]

What a leader feels at an emotional level is seen from her face and is perceived by the people around her. A recent neuroscience discovery is a system of "mirror neurons"[43], brain cells with the sole purpose of monitoring the behavior and emotions of others. Our brains are constantly scanning the environment, and we're tuned into people. High status people, such as leaders, get even more attention. The way a leader walks into the room affects the brains of everyone in the room.

That means "faking it" will fail. Pretending that everything is ok, if it is not, doesn't get you anywhere. Where the communication is unclear, or when there's a gap between what you say and what people perceive, interpretations will start to fly. Often the **real** meetings start in front of the coffee machine shortly after the one in the meeting room: "Did he seem off to you?" "There's something going on that we're not hearing." "Well, I got information from..."

If we want people to trust, if we want "resonance" and collaboration: Transparency is now a must-have. This doesn't mean that there's no longer confidentiality. Obviously, some data cannot be shared with everyone. We can, however, help people understand the mood we're in, and why.

Take Away:

We are not the great actors that we think we are, what's inside shows; while you can't share all the data, you can be honest about your feelings.

Examples of Transparency in Action

1. In meetings, how much time and energy is focused on "hiding" versus "sharing"? While there is data that must be confidential, much is not. Do leaders trust people with the truth?

2. Do your managers know enough about emotions and the neuroscience of leadership so they can make accurate decisions about what and how to share? Get them all substantive emotional intelligence training so they have understanding of the importance of self awareness, self management and self direction to create trustworthy relations – and the skills to make it happen.

3. Is emotional transparency the norm, or are your people expected to fake feelings? Every meeting, every performance review, every conversation is an opportunity to practice emotional transparency: "I am feeling _____, what about you?" Starting from emotions, especially in crucial conversations, creates a foundation of honesty and trust. This acknowledgement is key to transforming unpleasant feelings into pleasant feelings.

Coherence [Trust Pulse Point]

This concept applies at multiple levels, starting with our internal physiology: the rhythm of our heartbeat becomes more regular when we're in a state of energized calm, and less regular as we become reactive.[44] We're getting a biological signal when we're out of balance.[45]

Coherence also applies between what's inside and what's outside. If we believe XYZ are important, are we putting those values into action? Are we "walking the talk"? If not, we're sending a signal that we're not trustworthy.

At a leadership level, coherence affects change. According to the research we shared in INSIDE CHANGE[46], one of the most-frequently cited reasons for change-failure is that leaders are not actually modeling the change. They nod their heads, but they don't lead the way.

Finally, we can consider coherence in organizational systems. Are the systems and structures coherent with the organization's stated goals and values? If we say innovation is important, is our culture open to new ideas? If we say employees should be empowered, do we actually give them power? If we say success is about more than numbers, are we evaluating performance in a balanced scorecard?

In any of these levels, incoherence is a signal of chaos, or misalignment. This quickly creates untrustworthiness. Trust is an emotion, and when talking about emotions we need to remember a basic truth: perception is more real than reality. So perceived inconsistency will damage trust. Perceived inequity will be felt as distrust. We need to attend to the _feeling_ of coherence as a signal.

Take Away:

Set realistic expectations then follow them with great care; ensure there's an alignment between what's said and done – inside yourself, in your team, and across the organization.

Examples of Coherence in Action

1. Remember people do 70% of what you do and 30% of what you say to do. The only way to be credible as a leader is to be a role model. Unfortunately, no shortcuts are available.

2. Are you and others expecting people to be mind readers? Don't assume people have the information to understand why you do what you do. Take time to explain the reason why you are doing something, your emotional state and so on. What is clear to you, could be strange to others.

3. Are your leaders trying to deal with emotions by being rational? Remember, when it comes to emotion: Perception is more real than reality. One of your goals as a leader is to perceive the emotions around you to be sure that people really understand what you are doing and why. Emotions are information (though not from your brain's rational network), and this data provides insight into what's happening inside you and around you.

Care [Trust Pulse Point]

If trust is part of your measure of leadership effectiveness, then taking care of your people is one of your very top priorities. Research on the highest performing leaders shows that they balance care for the individual with care for the work.[47] They treat people-as-people, they value people not as a human "resource" but as a human being. Then they make space for those people to get important work done.

This has nothing to do with the leadership style. Different people express their care and concern in different ways based on style, experience, role, and the situation. Plus, there's no point in trying to "appear caring," as that destroys Transparency.

Note that this takes work. As John Gottman explained in a 2007 interview in HBR, leaders who are most effective at building relationships go out of their way: They make time to create small moments for caring.[48]

Caring about people means: let them perceive their importance inside the team. Listen instead of judging. Accept difference. Value the messiness. Commit: Give them your respect and support because they are people. It's not conditional, it's not something earned – it's something everyone gets just for coming in the door.

Take Away:

Care means giving unconditional regard and valuing people-as-people; this is the starting point for mutual trust.

Examples of Care in Action

1. Are people in your team actually kind to one another? Genuine kindness is likely more powerful than a whole catalog of corporate reward systems. Do you treat people with respect? Are you interested in their personal and professional development? Do you go out of your way to connect?

2. Are you working hard to guarantee a positive climate in your team? Often leaders prioritize tasks and systems and let "the people stuff" succeed or fail without attention: Leadership is a people business - and it takes work.

3. Is employee appreciation real, or an empty ritual? Genuine gratitude is felt. While some people like a special certificate or visible recognition, if appreciation doesn't start with caring, it's simply a transaction.

Recap

New technologies. New generations. New regulations. New priorities. So we should manage organizations following the rules created in 1950? It's time to pivot.

The five Vital Signs are powerful drivers of performance. So, for each Driver, we've defined a new rule of management. You've read why they're important, and "pulse points" to operationalize the new rules:

Driver	Pulse Points
Motivation from extrinsic to intrinsic motivation.	**Meaning:** create the Why **Mastery:** build on strengths **Autonomy:** give ownership
Teamwork from individual to team performance.	**Divergence:** seek contrasting views **Connection:** create common ground **Joy:** amplify emotional fuel
Execution from rigid to agile execution.	**Focus:** narrow attention to essentials **Accountability:** make results visible **Feedback:** create continuous awareness
Change from managing to inspiring change.	**Imagination:** create emotions for innovation **Exploration:** prototype & refine **Celebration:** learn & appreciate
Trust from demanding to earning trust.	**Transparency:** share more truth **Coherence:** walk the talk **Care:** foster genuine connections

Now it's time to see an example of what it means to put all these things together. In the next section we'll see what happened at Komatsu.

Part III

Vitality in Action - Case Study

In this chapter, we'll focus on a real example to illustrate how to use the new managerial rules we have seen. Of course we are not suggesting to replicate the case we'll describe, but to reflect on how you can embed the new rules in your management.

Increasing the Vital Signs at Komatsu

Is it possible to increase the Vital Signs? In a six month leadership development process at Komatsu all the five factors increased while plant performance also increased by 9.4%.

Background

株式会社小松製作所 (Kabushiki-gaisha Komatsu Seisakusho) is a Japanese multinational corporation that manufactures construction, mining, and military equipment, as well as industrial equipment like press machines, lasers and thermoelectric generators.[2] While headquarters are in Tokyo, the corporation was named after the city of Komatsu, Ishikawa, where the company was founded in 1921. The Japanese characters 小松 ko matsu mean "small pine tree," a symbol of the city.

Komatsu is the world's second largest manufacturer of construction equipment and mining equipment after Caterpillar. However, in some areas (Japan, China), Komatsu has a larger share than Caterpillar. It has manufacturing operations in Japan, Asia, Americas and Europe.

In Italy, Komatsu has a plant in Este for the construction of diggers; the Este plant is the focus of this case. The global recession significantly affected the plant's sales. The plant received a directive from Japan to prepare for the next opportunities that would arise post-recession, but in the recessionary climate, management faced serious struggles, including low engagement.

As Francesco Blasi, the HR Director, explains: "The project was in the midst of a period of crisis, including reduction in staff. In this difficult period, we still need to be able to team up and go forward. At the same time, it's important for us to identify and develop the people who can feed the next stage of the company's growth."

Blasi continues: "The decision to invest in an innovative project is inherent in the word crisis: as well as a time of difficulty, this should be a time of opportunity. Therefore, we felt it was necessary to change perspectives; to see our work from a new angle. We wanted to involve our key personnel in a methodology that would allow us to escape from the usual patterns."

In April 2012, Komatsu partnered with Six Seconds to increase the engagement of people in order to build competitive capability and create a case demonstrating the plant's commitment for innovation. The project blended assessments, training, and project-based learning to involve managers in creating a context for innovation. The project focused on 24 second-line managers.

The project was designed using the Change MAP[49], the model we have briefly seen in the first section, an iterative process for organizational transformation. The Change MAP follows three phases:

Engage: Build buy-in

Activate: Develop new capabilities.

Reflect: Lock-in wins.

The phases of the Komatsu project included:

Engage

Team Vital Signs (TVS) for managers

1-day project launch + training

Activate

Vital Team pilot:

- Team creation
- 3x progress meetings
- 3x team meetings
- Distance learning

Reflect

Feedback surveys

TVS post-test

1-day conference

Tools

Two assessments were used in the program; an individual measure of emotional intelligence, and group assessment of the vital SIgns.

Emotional Intelligence

Emotional Intelligence was measured with the Six Seconds Emotional Intelligence Assessment (SEI).[50] The SEI is based on the Six Seconds Model of Emotional Intelligence consisting of eight core competencies divided into three macro areas:

> Self Awareness, called "Know Yourself" includes two competencies: Enhance Emotional Literacy and Recognize Patterns.

> Self Management, called "Choose Yourself" includes four competencies: Apply Consequential Thinking, Navigate Emotions, Engage Intrinsic Motivation, Exercise Optimism.

> Self Direction, called "Give Yourself," includes two competencies: Increase Empathy and Pursue Noble Goals.

The assessment provides an overall EQ score plus scores for each of the three macro areas and each of the eight competencies for a total of 12 normative values.

In this project we have used two reports from the SEI toolset:

BBP: Brain Brief Profile – this tool identifies "Brain Style," the individual's current tendency for processing emotional and cognitive data. BBP is designed as an engaging, quick, meaningful starting point for developing emotional intelligence

GR: Group Report – this profile shows distributions of EQ competencies. It is designed for program planning, and for coaching/training team leaders

Team Vital Signs

People Engagement was measured with TVS (Team Vital Signs), a statistically reliable research process designed to pinpoint areas assisting and interfering with growth and bottom-line success.

As previously discussed, the Vital Signs model consists of five key drivers: Trust, Motivation, Change, Teamwork, and Execution.

The Team Vital Signs is a measure for intact workgroups. The assessment generates normative scores for each factor on a scale from 50-150 with 100 as the mean.

An additional scale in the TVS is a measure of engagement, which represents an overall view of the participants' commitment to the organization. The "Engagement Index" is based on ratio of the number of employees who are actively engaged (fully committed) vs neutral vs disengaged (not committed). The Engagement Index is reported on a scale from 0 to 100%, with 50% as a mean score.

Intervention

As explained, the program design follows the Change MAP, Six Seconds' framework for transformation:

> The **Engage** phase focuses on creating readi-

ness, and included pre-assessment and initial training.

The **Activate** phase focuses on building capability, and included additional training and individual coaching.

The **Reflect** phase is about solidifying learning, and included post-assessment and evaluation.

In total, the program included 30 hours of in-person work for each group, some distance learning activities and reflections, plus some assignments to be done between one meeting and the other.

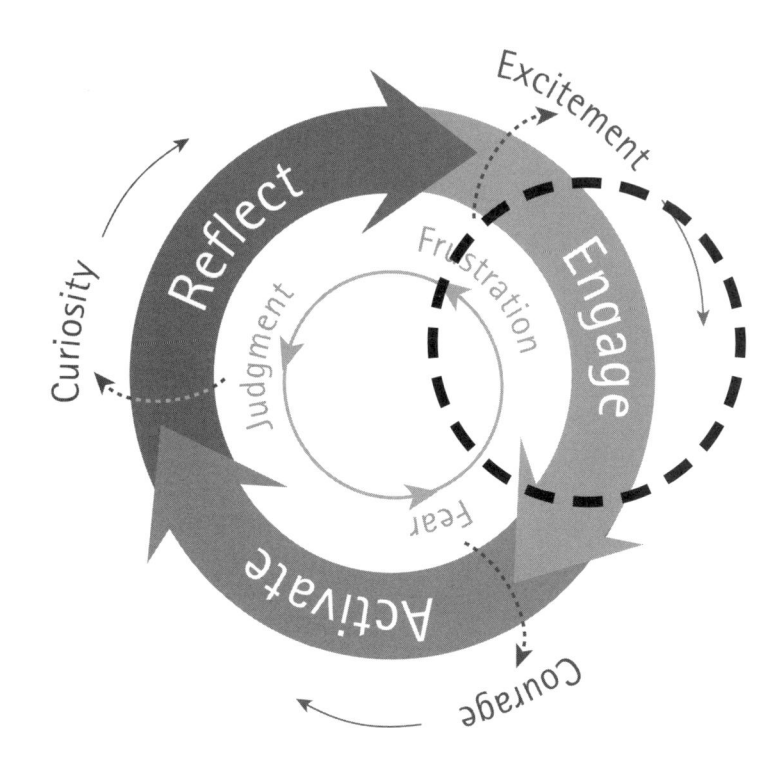

Engage

This phase began with meetings with the HR department and communication with the senior management team to identify a clear set of goals. Next steps included assessments and meetings with the management team to review results, then to create and launch a plan.

Team Vital Signs

The preliminary assessment revealed a significant challenge in employee engagement. Only 8.3% of the management team scored in the "Engaged" category. The overall "Engagement Index" score was 33% (the mean score on this index is 50%; the benchmark for high performance is 80%).

The pre-program scores on the five factors of the TVS assessment are shown in the graphic below.

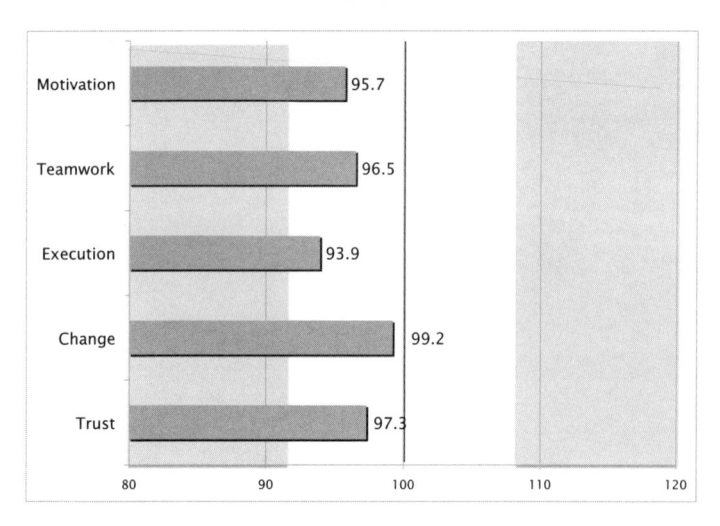

Motivation	95.7
Teamwork	96.5
Execution	93.9
Change	99.2
Trust	97.3

All the factors were below the mean (100), but looking at the relative strengths and weaknesses, there are signals of a readiness to change. The challenge was to immediately realize results in order to support people to re-engage and see that it is possible to deliver value.

The other key concern was about trust: Given the business situation, it's not difficult to understand why managers felt concern – but it was clear that we had to do as much as possible to create a feeling of safety and a real inside-out commitment for change to occur.

The TVS also includes an indicator of coherence of responses. Fortunately, in this case the people were highly aligned about the situation, indicating a shared perspective.

Management Meeting

The management team met with Six Seconds' facilitators to review the TVS results. The meeting focused on confronting current reality and clarifying a vision of the future [Motivation pulse point: Meaning]. Facilitators emphasized why it is important to work on the engagement of people especially in a time of uncertainty

The dialogue was constructive and participants focused on how to move forward. The meeting emphasized three key points:

1. The current situation is not sustainable [Trust pulse point: Transparency].

2. The plant needs to be ready for new opportunities

[Execution pulse point: Accountability].

3. The management team can influence the future [Motivation pulse point: Autonomy].

The next stages of the project were outlined:

- Training for 2nd-line managers in the afternoon.
- Explanation of the Vital Team process.
- Volunteers join the Vital Team process and implement.
- Repeat of the TVS.

Francesco Blasi explains key success factors in this process:

> "The second line management was already informed of the activities that had previously carried out the first line, and consequently were aware of the overall methodology. In the kick-off meeting, the senior leaders were present, although they were not directly involved in the dialogue [Care, pulse point Trust]. However, they were expected to give their support, their sponsorship, together with the Managing Director.

It was essential that the 2nd-line managers knew that if they volunteered for the projects, they would have backing from their leaders" [Trust pulse point: Coherence].

Management Training

In the afternoon all the second line managers attended an action learning training [Teamwork pulse point: Connection] to begin developing new insights and tools to address their challenges. The training topics included:

1. How people work: Insights on motivation, collaboration, and engagement.

2. The Brain: The value of emotions + rationality working together.

3. Change: The Change MAP process as a framework for workplace performance.

Finally, the end of the day focused on the **Vital Team process**. This is a methodology Six Seconds uses to initiate change. The methodology involves teams working on concrete projects for a limited time (usually 90 days or less).

Three key objectives [Execution pulse point: Focus] were presented:

- Increase engagement of people.
- Learn and practice new skills in a "hands on" process.
- Increase value for people - through people.

The managers were invited to volunteer for the process [Motivation pulse point: Autonomy]. As the HR Director said:

> "It was very important for people to be able to choose whether or not to participate in the next step of the project. If someone wanted to stay out, no problem. We were giving an opportunity to people and we only wanted to include those who were convinced about the value of this effort. The managers' Initial reaction was a great deal of curiosity, careful consideration of expectations, and then, above all, a lot of enthusiasm."

In the end, all of the managers elected to join this project and went onto the Activate phase.

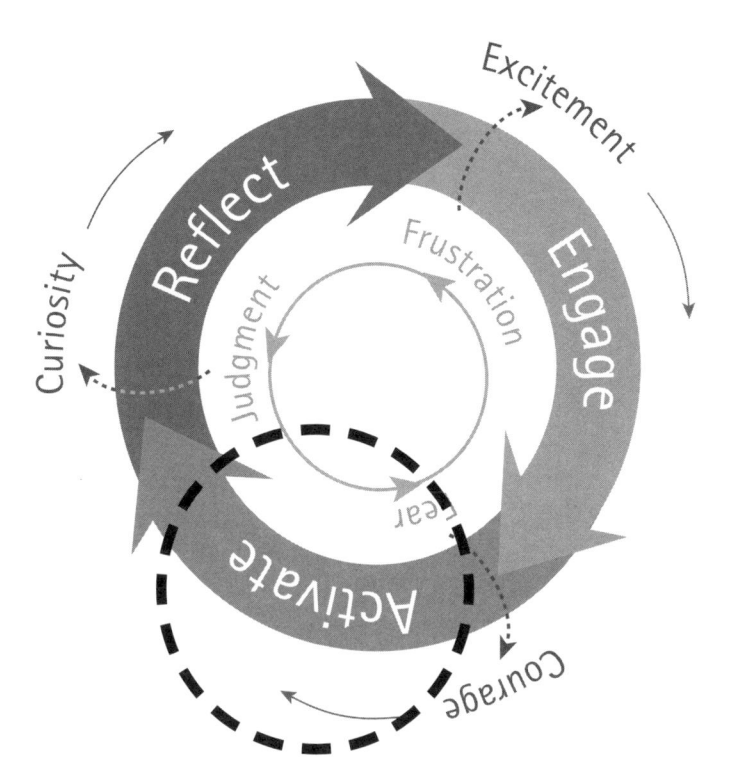

Activate

In this phase, project groups were created using Six Seconds' "Vital Team" methodology. Then, following the Change MAP process, teams worked to create value for people, through people.

Vital Teams

The Vital Team process was used to form three small groups for the pilot projects. The goal is a team that's divergent but also aligned, balanced but also dynamic. The process includes:

Skills: Review of curriculum vitae of each person to make sure necessary job skills were present in each group.

EQ: Measure emotional intelligence using the SEI assessment to create a mix of competencies and Brain Styles.

Organizational Roles: Each participant answered a brief questionnaire about roles that people have within the organization. The survey identifies who are the leaders for passing information, strategic advice, technical and operational support, new ideas and unconventional thinking, personal connections and role modeling.

Three teams were formed to maximize the level of diversity [Teamwork pulse point: Divergence] in terms of Brain Style, leadership, competences and skills. This method is based on a belief that divergence is a pre-condition for innovation. The opportunity to see current reality from different points of view is one of the competitive advantages of a team.

In the Vital Signs framework there are three key ingredients of change: Imagination, Exploration and Celebration. The team meetings were structured around these elements:

Imagination

All the project teams met together in a plenary session for an hour to review the goal [Execution pulse point: Focus]: **Create value for people, through people** – and to explain the stages of the project. Then, each small group met for two hours with a facilitator for an engaging session with plenty of humor [Teamwork pulse point: Joy].

The first two-hour meeting included:

- Present SEI Group Report in order to start thinking about the dynamics that we could experience working together, discuss about how we can use the strengths [Motivation pulse point: Mastery] of the members to be an high performing team.

- Imagine what an organization has to do to really improve the value for people. Create metaphors for a highly people-centered company. Consider what other organizations (in every sector - business, sport, not for profit) already do [Change pulse point: Imagination].

- Define metrics of success at the end of the project.

Assignments were given to:

- Read excerpts from INSIDE CHANGE focused on engaging people in change.

- Research their own and other organizations to see how they engage people [Execution pulse point: Accountability].

Exploration

Again, a Six Seconds' facilitator led an hour-long plenary meeting of all teams to check-in on the process. This was followed by a 2-hour meeting of each team.

The second day meeting started with a review of the assignments. Next, the groups each identified at least three practical ideas of what they could do now in Komatsu to leverage the value for people. At the end of the session, each group had agreed on one idea to pursue.

Team 1: Knowledge Sharing.

This group designed internal training courses to explain the various business functions in Komatsu and share who does what within the organization. To enhance understanding of the business' purpose, each employee would have a chance to try the machines the plant builds.

Team 2: Service Desk.

Group two planned a process where internal and external experts could help employees with various needs (such as financial planning, tax consulting, insurance and bank assistance).

Team 3: Performance Assessment.

This group decided to revise the internal performance management system to create more participation. They developed a "360" feedback process to include supervisors, colleagues, and co-workers in performance appraisal.

Assignments were given to:

- Create a prototype plan of the project [Change pulse point: Exploration] and then collect input on the plan [Execution pulse point: Feedback].

- Read a collection of articles and tips from www.6seconds.org that were emailed weekly about team projects.

Celebration

The third meeting started with a presentation of the prototype to the HR Director to obtain a formal "ok" to go ahead with the experiment [Trust pulse point: Transparency].

Next, the teams revised their plans and prepared for a presentation to the first line managers, which was the plenary session at the end of the day; the senior managers paid very close attention to recognize the care and attention to the work [Change pulse point: Celebration].

The next month was dedicated to the trial of the prototypes.

Francesco Blasi's comment on the process:

> "The teams showed great enthusiasm and really wanted to achieve the goal. The initial enthusiasm was also fueled

a healthy rivalry between the groups. There was a strong team spirit within each group and very positive energy was created."

Reflect

After the month-long pilot of the three projects, the Reflect phase included surveys to employees to give feedback about the three projects, a repeat of the TVS assessment [Execution pulse point: Feedback], and a final conference with all managers.

In the post-assessment of the TVS, as shown below, the there was a dramatic improvement in engagement.

All employees at the plant were invited to give feedback on the three projects through a brief, anonymous survey as "internal customers" of the three projects. The employee survey showed around 90% customer satisfaction, with the "Service Desk" winning the highest ratings. These high

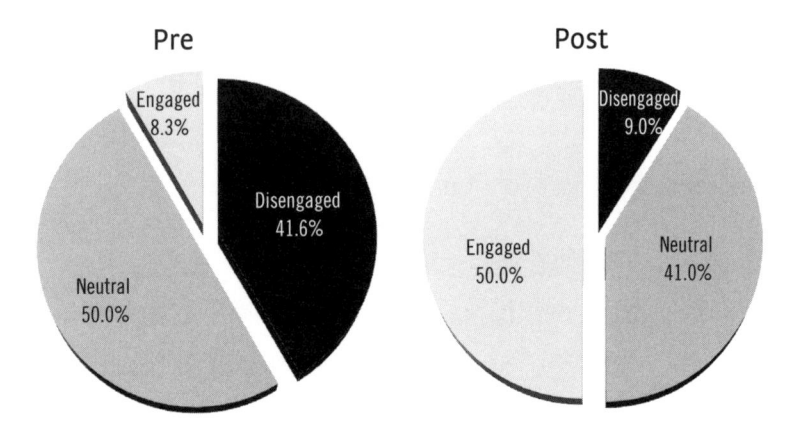

Pre
- Engaged 8.3%
- Disengaged 41.6%
- Neutral 50.0%

Post
- Disengaged 9.0%
- Engaged 50.0%
- Neutral 41.0%

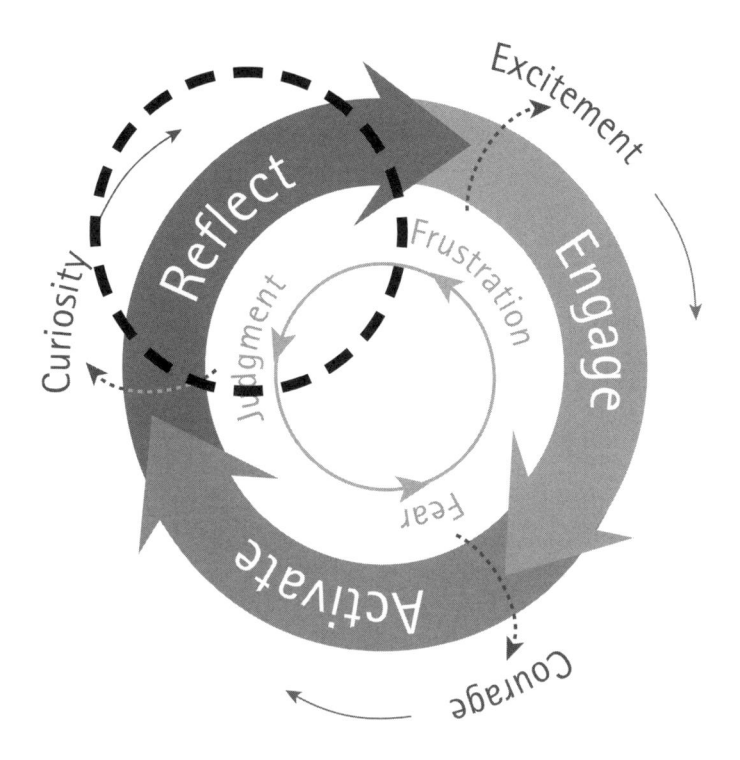

scores are a signal that the managers did, in fact, create value for people – through people.

Results

In post-assessment of managers on Team Vital Signs, the overall engagement index increased from 33% to 70%. The percentage of people in the "Engaged" category shifted from just over 8% on the pre-test, to 50% on the post-test. At the same time, the percentage of disengaged dropped from 41.6% to 9%, representing a large-scale shift in attitude.

Meanwhile, the plant's efficiency scores (calculated based on factory output and cost) improved by 9.4%, demonstrating an important link between increased engagement and the bottom line.

Results on each scale also improved dramatically, as shown in this graphic, where post-test scores are in bold:

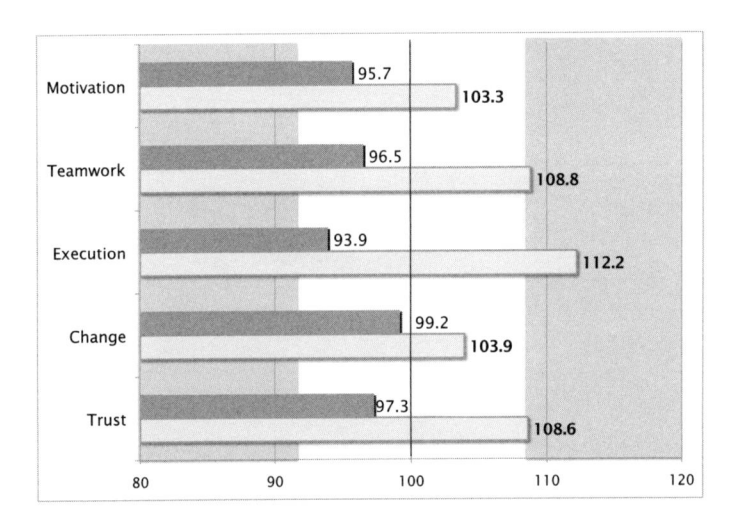

Scale	Pre	Post
Motivation	95.7	103.3
Teamwork	96.5	108.8
Execution	93.9	112.2
Change	99.2	103.9
Trust	97.3	108.6

Blasi summarizes the results as follows:

> "The key lesson is in the approach used. Managers in the project experienced something new, and then, on their own initiative, they started to utilize the method in communicating and man-

> aging their employees. This is the real test of any training: Do people start to use what they learned? Now we need to spread this methodology to a wider audience, but certainly it's clear that things have changed for the better."

One specific example Blasi identified is the contagious effect of a positive team experience. "Looking at the environment in the trainings, people felt good – it was practical, but also warm. They then worked to re-create this experience for others. And, in my opinion an added value, we can definitely see that for many people involved, the word 'emotion' is no longer taboo."

The study is based on a small group of managers, but it shows that effective teamwork has a significant effect on the larger community. Using an "emotionally intelligent" process for building and supporting teams seems to work.

Blasi concluded:

> "First of all, a very banal lesson: if you do something you can obtain results, but if you do nothing definitely you will not get anything.
>
> Every change is a risk, and taking about

a 'taboo' subject such as emotions in a very technical organization does seem like a risk! But it's a basic idea: if we have people staying in their comfortable culture, they will not think differently. We need to ask them questions and to allow them to see from a different point of view. This provides another lens for them to see their everyday behaviors.

I am not saying all, but many have understood this and are starting to realize that they have an impact on their people. Emotions are real, even if you can't touch them or see them… they touch others in a powerful way. For me, this awareness is the revolutionary thing that has happened."

The Vital Lessons

To summarize, the Komatsu project demonstrates a Vital Organization:

1. **Meaning** - we started with the Vision and at each step we underlined why we were doing this kind of project. The overall idea was to keep the Este Plant

alive and show to the Japanese management that the people in Italy were committed and ready to innovate. It was a way to maintain hope in the future of the plant.

2. **Mastery** - we continuously emphasized the importance to start from strengths. Every time there was a new step we asked a question such as, "Who wants to be in charge of the planning, who is strong at that?" Of course, starting from strengths also lowers the anxiety of change.

3. **Autonomy** - When people self-select, they have power. They become more committed to the process, and they feel ownership of the results. This is why we asked people to chose if they want to be considered for the project. We have given them choice to do or not to do. Really.

4. **Divergence** - We used a methodology to maximize the level of divergence inside each group and we explained that to all the participants. This was great to permit people in different areas to know other people and create the possibility to think outside the box with different perspective at the table.

5. **Connection** - each session started with a team challenge. During the facilitations we frequently underlined the power of connection using the emotional intelligence tools to show people what it means to have a real connection with other people. Of course the opportunity to stay together during meetings and to prepare for the projects created the base to build connection.

6. **Joy** - you cannot create innovative learning through suffering. The brain, to learn at its best, needs engaging emotions and to set the right mood for learning. As facilitators, we started by asking ourselves: what am I feeling before the class? As usual emotions are contagious. Then we used videos or exercise or surprise in each meeting to maintain fun and humor.

7. **Focus** - the goals were clear, the CEO presented it, the HR manager underlined it. Each session, every facilitator did the same at the beginning and at the end of each session. And by, the way, we measured it.

8. **Accountability** - we were facilitators, not controllers; we left the responsibility for the work to the teams. They identified a leader and they decided how to divide work between them. At the end, they were responsible for the results. We didn't call the leader the evening before to check if the planned work was done.

9. **Feedback** - we maintained, from the beginning, an obsessive attention to feedback. We started with the TVS, then collecting people's comments on the prototypes (from within the groups and from internal clients of the services), the HR manager gave his feedback and each facilitator shared a lot of feedback during the in-person sessions. Finally, at the end, another round of TVS. So frequent, brief, real-time data.

10. **Imagination** - a consistent part of the first small group activity was dedicated to think outside the

box, without constraints and barriers. *How would you imagine an organization capable of creating value to people? What are examples of this anywhere in the world?* The point was to try to exit from a narrow boundary of examples from competitors and find inspiration in different sectors, not only business oriented, but not-for-profit too. Imagination is the way we can see beyond our patterns.

11. **Exploration** - the whole project was built to quickly to test many ideas by creating prototypes; this real-world testing makes the implications visible. From this activity, all the teams discovered new insights about their ideas and refined the projects multiple times to make it more effective. By the way, seeing these improvements created new energy to go even further with refining.

12. **Celebration** - as facilitators, we dedicated time in each session to reflect about what worked and what didn't work. We acknowledged and valued the process of learning. In addition, we scheduled formal moments (the presentation to the HR manager, the plenary meetings and the final presentation to the management) as a way to share progress.

13. **Transparency** - from the beginning, the CEO spoke frankly about the reasons for this project: "We are on a burning platform and we want to try to influence our future." There was no effort to hide the risks, rather, a willingness to confront the difficulty and pain of this moment. That honesty created

resonance and started people moving. People felt the truth in his words and emotions, and decided to try to influence their future.

14. **Coherence** - in Blasi's final comments, he mentions that the managers turned around and started treating people in the organization the way they had been treated in this project – that's the power of coherence. We tried to carefully walk the talk as facilitators. At a strategic level, the project also showed coherence between the company's goals and the individual managers; they were creating organizational value in a way that was tangible and aligned to their personal values.

15. **Care** - the overall project was launched because Komatsu cared about the future of the people. All the leaders were at the first meeting to give a sign of commitment and re-assure their people. Senior managers dedicated their own time, and gave manager's time for personal and professional development (e.g., with the emotional intelligence reports and the frequent debriefings about what was going on). It was not a surprise that at the end of the project lots of people start using the same methodology with their collaborators.

Do you see other vital lessons?

Recap

The Komatsu case shows that these "new rules for management" are not some abstract, esoteric ideas. Every day at the office, you have numerous opportunities to apply the pulse points.

Our hope is that by tuning into the new rules, and seeing this practical example, you'll begin to see the opportunities everywhere. Then, as you begin to shift your own and your organization's management practice, you'll quickly see the power of working WITH people – of aligning your leadership to the way the human brain really works.

Ultimately, the point is vitality. Tapping human energy to create a flourishing workplace – that's more efficient and profitable while contributing meaningful value to all the stakeholders.

Endnotes

1   State of the Global Workplace http://www.gallup.com/strategicconsulting/164735/state-global-workplace.aspx

2   On 9/1/14, searching for the term "performance management" in the Books category: 63,974 results.

3   For example, see Gen. George Casey (2014) "Leading in a VUCA World," Fortune (http://fortune.com/2014/03/20/leading-in-a-vuca-world/)

4   Freedman, Fariselli, Ghini (2011) Vital Signs Technical Manual, Six Seconds.

5   Daniel Kahneman - Facts. Nobelprize.org. www.nobelprize.org/nobel_prizes/economic-sciences/laureates/2002/kahneman-facts.html

6   If you want an updated version of Kahneman's theory you can read Thinking Fast and Slow, Farrar, Straus and Giroux, 2010

7   Henry Mintzberg, The nature of managerial work, Harpercollins College Div, 1973.

8   There is a terrific New York Times article from the Nobel winning economist Paul Krugman about that How Did Economists Get It So Wrong? http://www.nytimes.com/2009/09/06/magazine/06Economic-t.html

9   For a simple and effective description on how our brains work see Daniel Goleman, Emotional Intelligence, Bantam, 1995.

10   LeDoux, Joseph (2003), The Emotional Brain, Fear, and the Amygdala (Cellular and Molecular Neurobiology)

11   Candace Pert (2007), "The Physics of Emotion," http://www.6seconds.org/2007/01/26/the-physics-of-emotion-candace-pert-on-feeling-good/

12   Salovey, P., & Mayer, J.D. (1990). Emotional intelligence. Imagination, Cognition, and Personality, 9, 185-211.

13   Freedman (2012) At the Heart of Leadership.

14   Robert Ingram, presentation at the Six Seconds Conference, 2008

15   Joshua Freedman (2012) At the Heart of Leadership, Six Seconds

16   Woolfold & Allen (2007) Treating Somatization: A Cognitive-behavioral Approach, Guilford Press

17   Caruso & Salovey (2004), The Emotionally Intelligent Manager, John Wiley & Sons

18   Barsade, S.G., & Gibson, D.E. (2007). Why does affect matter in organizations? Academy of Management Perspectives, 36-59.

19   Paul Ekman (2007), Emotions Revealed, Macmillan

20   De Martino, Kumaran, Seymour, Dolan, Frames, Biases and Rational Decision-Making in the Human Brain, Science, vol.313, pag 684-687, 2006.

21   Kin Fai Ellick Wong, Jessica Yuk Yee Kwong, Carmen K. Ng (2008) "When Thinking Rationally Increases Bi-

ases: The Role of Rational Thinking Style in Escalation of Commitment," Applied Psychology

22   In addition, the Six Seconds Emotional Intelligence test, SEI, measures these capabilities and the eight underlying competencies that enable these three pursuits.

23   Freedman (2011), "The Neuroscience of Chai," http://www.6seconds.org/2011/01/31/neuroscience-chai-obstinance/

24   Kotter, John P. (1996), Leading Change, Harvard Business School Press

25   William Bridges (2009), Managing Transitions: Making the Most of Change, Da Capo Press

26   Freedman & Ghini (2010), INSIDE CHANGE, Six Seconds Press

27   Victor Vroom (1964), Work and Motivation, Wiley

28   Daniel Pink (2011), Drive: The Surprising Truth About What Motivates Us, Penguin

29   Paul Valéry (1937) from "Notre Destin et Les Lettres," "L'avenir est comme le reste: il n'est plus ce qu'il était."

30   Richard Wiseman (2009), 59 Seconds: Think a Little, Change a Lot, Borzoi Books

31   Candace Pert (2007), "The Physics of Emotions" (http://www.6seconds.org/2007/01/26/the-physics-of-emotion-candace-pert-on-feeling-good/)

32   Baba Shiv (2013), "How Do You Find Breakthrough Ideas?"   (http://www.gsb.stanford.edu/news/headlines/baba-shiv-how-do-you-find-breakthrough-ideas)

Also see Ryan Underwood (2014), "Using Neuroscience to Boost Your Creativity" in INC. (http://www.inc.com/magazine/201402/ryan-underwood/creativity-boosters-neuroscience.html)

33   Joshua Freedman (2013), "Don't Settle for Happiness,"   (http://www.6seconds.org/2013/07/26/dont-settle-for-happiness/)

34   Holweg, Matthias (2007). "The genealogy of lean production." Journal of Operations Management 25 (2): 420–437.

35   A tricolon is a three-part rhetorical device widely used in speeches: "We came, we saw, we conquered." "Life, liberty, and the pursuit of happiness."

36   This is one of the important findings from our latest research on leaders, summarized here: www.6seconds.org/2014/06/04/talking-about-great-leaders/

37   The US military uses this acronym for Volatile, Uncertain, Complex, Ambiguous situations, see "What really makes the difference in uncertain times?" in Part I

38   According to the Manpower Group 2013 Talent Shortage Survey, 35% of employers globally are having trouble filling positions, see www.manpowergroup.us/campaigns/talent-shortage-2013/

39 Pally, R. (2007). The Predicting Brain: Unconscious Repetition, Conscious Reflection and Therapeutic Change. International Journal of Psychoanalysis

40 See INSIDE CHANGE in Part I

41 Clayton M. Christensen (2000), The Innovator's Dilemma, HarperBusiness

42 Baba Shiv (2013), "How Do You Find Breakthrough Ideas?" (http://www.gsb.stanford.edu/news/headlines/baba-shiv-how-do-you-find-breakthrough-ideas)

43 Giacomo Rizzolatti and Corrado Sinigaglia, Mirrors in the brain, Oxford University Press, 2008

44 Jos Vander Sloten et al (2009), "Influence of Mental Stress on Heart Rate and Heart Rate Variability," 4th European Conference of the International Federation for Medical and Biological Engineering, Springer

45 The Institute of HeartMath has catalogued extensive research on this topic, for a summary see http://www.heartmath.org/research/science-of-the-heart/

46 Freedman & Ghini (2010), INSIDE CHANGE, Six Seconds Press, pages 6-16

47 Analysis of thousands of high performing leaders compared to average performers reveals that one of the top differentiators is "tough empathy," caring blended with business focus. See "Talking About Great Leaders" on www.6seconds.org

48   Diane Coutu (2007) Making Relationships Work: A Conversation with Psychologist John M. Gottman, Harvard Business Review (http://www.6seconds.org/2007/12/12/hbr-john-gottman-on-making-relationships-work/)

49   Freedman & Ghini (2012) INSIDE CHANGE. Also see "Structuring Transformational Learning" on www.6seconds.org

50   The only tool based on Six Seconds' model, the SEI is focused on developing key capacities for living and leading with emotional intelligence. (www.6seconds.org)

About the Authors

Massimiliano Ghini, MBA, is the Director of the Center for Innovative Management. A professor of Human Resources Management and People Management at Alma Graduate School (AGS), the Business School of the University of Bologna. At AGS Max is in charge of Organization and Personnel of the Professional MBA.

Max's author credits include *INSIDE CHANGE*, the *People Management Toolbox*, the *Six Seconds Emotional Intelligence Assessment (SEI)*, the *Vital Signs* assessments, plus numerous articles and white papers on EQ and business performance. His research, articles and findings were published in Fortune, Ilsole24ore, and Direzione del Personale.

Joshua Freedman is the CEO of Six Seconds, and one of the world's leading specialists on developing and applying emotional intelligence to improve performance. A leader, author, and educator, Freedman takes hard science and makes it applicable.

For over a decade he has helped lead the emotional intelligence network, developing offices around the globe; top practitioners and researchers; renown scientists and leaders as advisory board members; and award-winning materials including seven validated assessment tools.

Joshua is the author of *At the Heart of Leadership*, a practical guide for leaders to tap the power of emotions to get better results, as well as numerous assessment and development tools to improve the people-side of performance.

About Six Seconds

Six Seconds is a global network supporting people to create positive change - everywhere, all the time. Our experience and research shows that the skills of emotional intelligence (EQ) are invaluable for leading change. Therefore, we conduct research, develop powerful measures and tools for EQ development, and support a world-wide network of experts to put the learnable, measurable skills of emotional intelligence into action.

Our vision is that by 2039, one billion people will be practicing the skills of emotional intelligence.

For more information, see www.6seconds.org/about.

Six Seconds' Founder, Karen McCown, authored a method for integrating emotional and academic development, called *Self-Science*, first published in 1978. In 1995, Daniel Goleman described the Self-Science process as one of two models for teaching emotional intelligence. Established as a 501(c)3 organization in California in 1997, Six Seconds is now a global network with offices and representatives in 25 countries.